THE 5 PRACTICES *of the* CARING MENTOR

Strengthening the Mentoring Relationship from the Inside Out

Daniel H. Shapiro, EdD

Teacher and School Counselor Edition

PRAISE FOR

THE 5 PRACTICES *of the* CARING MENTOR

"The only thing more valuable than Dr. Daniel H. Shapiro's wisdom is his heart. In this invaluable guide, he not only points the way to the most successful mentoring relationship, but he also demonstrates how such relationships must feel. This book should be required reading for anyone who wants to help a colleague, student, or anyone at all!"

—Raphael Cushnir, author of *The One Thing Holding You Back: Unleashing the Power of Emotional Connection*

"Dr. Daniel H. Shapiro's first book, *The 5 Practices of the Caring Mentor: Strengthening the Mentoring Relationship from the Inside Out*, is a must-have resource for any educational leader, counseling professional, or teacher who intends to develop meaningful relationships with their mentors/mentees. True to his style, Dr. Shapiro writes in a way that engages and easily connects with the reader. This book will serve as an inspired guide to supervisors and mentors, both in the field of education and counseling, who wish to invest in their mentee's long-term professional and personal success."

—Dr. Melissa A. Mariani, co-author of *Facilitating Evidenced-Based, Data-Driven School Counseling: A Manual for Practice*

"Dr. Daniel H. Shapiro has authored an eloquently written and in-depth work about mentoring that will remind readers about the essential dynamics of work in schools with adults and students. *The 5 Practices of the Caring Mentor* offers readers a blend of the passion for mentoring, framed around creating authentic caring relationships, and integrated within evidence-based practices. Inspiring and informative, school counselors, teachers, and administrators will find this book a must read and a book to have in their professional libraries."

—Dr. Rebecca A. Schumacher, Executive Director, Florida School Counselor Association

"Dr. Shapiro provides the reader real-life application of effective strategies and practices to create a trusted mentor/mentee relationship for counselors and educators. This award-winning educator and counselor shares guidance both practical and heartfelt for developing a strong, trusting mentor/mentee partnership. Dr. Shapiro's outstanding book will become a powerful tool in the hands of all educators who serve as mentors."

—Catherine Kuhns, M.Ed, Broward County Math Teacher of the Year and Recipient of the Presidential Award for Excellence in Mathematics and Science Teaching

THE 5 PRACTICES *of the* CARING MENTOR

CONTENTS

PREFACE

I n more than twenty years as a teacher, school counselor, and educational leader, I've had extensive experience as a mentor. I've been a mentee and a mentor many times over—both as a teacher and a school counselor. For several years I have served as a district coordinator of mentoring for school counselors. I also wrote my doctoral dissertation on the subject of mentoring and conducted extensive individual interviews, focus groups, and document analyses.

As I reflect on my experiences, as well as the experiences of others, I find that the skills needed for successful teacher mentoring relationships are the same skills needed for successful school counselor mentoring relationships. The most important skill, however, that teachers and school counselors can develop in order to maximize their positive impact on mentees is the ability to care effectively.

I'm convinced that genuine, caring human connections form the foundation for mentoring relationships in the educational realm to grow and thrive. I see time and again the ways in which caring mentors bring out the best in mentees who are teachers and school counselors, meeting their social, emotional, and professional needs while helping them succeed in their work with students. On the other hand, I observe that when mentors do not express compassion within their mentoring relationships, mentees feel disconnected, unwelcomed, and unsupported in their efforts to establish themselves in their new roles. To have the greatest impact, a mentor must develop and maintain caring relationships with their mentees.

When, fresh out of college, I began my career as a physical education teacher, my first interview was for a position at an inner-city elementary school. At the time, I looked as if I were about twelve years old, so I dressed in my most mature-looking suit and made a mental note to deepen my voice as I spoke. On the day of the interview, I walked into the conference room, smiled, extended my hand, and introduced myself to Mrs. Franklin, one of the school's administrators, who conducted the interview. I felt as if the conversation went well, but at the end, Mrs. Franklin's brow crinkled as if to say, *You're really sweet, but you're not cut out to handle the tough situations you'll encounter at this school.*

Sensing Mrs. Franklin's hesitation to hire a brand-new teacher such as myself, especially one who looked as young as I did, I nodded slowly, thanked her for the interview, and walked out of the conference room. But, as I stepped through the door, something told me to turn around. I spun on my heel, looked Mrs. Franklin in the eye, and said, "I know I look young and don't have much experience, but if you give me a chance, I won't let you down." The next day, the phone rang. When I answered, Mrs. Franklin uttered five words I'll never forget. "Everyone deserves a chance, Daniel." In that moment, Mrs. Franklin took me under her wing and became my first educational mentor.

1st mentor

I arrived for the first day of school wearing a freshly pressed coaching shirt and carrying a shiny new clipboard and an oversized stack of notes about teaching physical education. I had planned my opening lesson well in advance and was ready for a successful start to my teaching career. My first class was a lively group of fifth graders. We met under a small shelter near the basketball court where I greeted the students, explained the class rules, and provided instructions for the day's activities. Before long, the students were engaged and cooperating with one another. One group was jumping rope in the shade, another was hula hooping in the freshly cut grass, and a third was doing drills on the basketball court. I stepped back and watched the class with a smile. Everyone was on task, performing the assigned skills just as I had taught them. So far, my first day was a success.

Then it came time to clean up. I blew my whistle and shouted directions. Most of the students returned their equipment and formed a line to reenter the building. A group of the bigger boys, however, decided to keep shooting hoops. *Maybe they didn't hear me*, I thought. So I raised my voice, asking them in a friendly but firm way to bring in the basketballs. Still, they kept playing.

Now all of the other students were watching. I knew I had to assert my authority in order to establish myself as a respected teacher. I demanded, in my strongest and most professional tone, that the students follow my directions. The boys and I locked eyes.

Standoff.

Then, as if in protest, they reared back and launched all of the basketballs onto the school's roof before joining the other students in line.

After school, Mrs. Franklin called me into her office to ask about my first day, one of the many ways she expressed how much she cared. I explained that things didn't exactly get off to the best start. Mrs. Franklin said, "Of course it was a little rough, Daniel. Every new teacher struggles during the first few days of school." I thanked her but added, "I'm not sure you understand, Mrs. Franklin, all of your basketballs are on the roof!"

Mrs. Franklin laughed, almost spilling her coffee, then became serious. "You can't expect to come into a new school community and just start teaching, Daniel. You have to get to know the students and let the students get to know you. You have to build real relationships with the children and families. You have to become a part of the community and show them you're someone they can trust."

I took the long way home that afternoon, thinking about Mrs. Franklin's words. The next morning, I positioned myself at the school's front door and welcomed every student and family member as he or she arrived. I walked children home after school, attended community events, and served as a volunteer coach at the local park where many of our students played youth football. As I came to know my students and their families better, I began to care deeply for them, and I realized they also cared for me. Discipline issues in my classes became rare, and soon I was doing much better as a teacher.

Mrs. Franklin continued to check in with me each week, practicing what she preached by taking the time to get to know me, learn about my family, and ask about my life and career goals. Of course, she also asked how my lessons were proceeding and helped me reflect on my instructional practice, but she always started by expressing her interest in me as a person. With patience and understanding, Mrs. Franklin gave me the support I needed as a young man and new teacher, never failing to offer a compassionate ear and words of encouragement after a tough day.

I'd always believed in giving my best, but Mrs. Franklin's caring approach made me want to work even harder. She showed me what it meant for an established educator to commit to mentoring a new teacher with an emphasis on a caring relationship. Ms. Franklin saw I had the potential to succeed. She knew a caring mentor would be an essential aspect of my growth and decided to give me a chance.

Under Mrs. Franklin's guidance, I learned how to manage and instruct my classes, and I even supported other new teachers myself from time to time. I learned firsthand the value of strong relationships, and ever since, I have made it my priority to put the human connection with students, families, and colleagues at the forefront of everything I do.

I wrote this book because, although mentoring programs may be developed with the best of intentions, they will not be effective without a strong foundation of care. New teachers and school counselors need more than to be instructed on standards, procedures, and techniques. As Mrs. Franklin taught me, teachers and school counselors need the support of mentors who care and who are well equipped to express that compassion in ways that benefit their mentees.

When I reflect on my life and career, I don't treasure the accomplishments, awards, or good opinions of others. Instead, what mean the most to me are the moments of genuine presence, the opportunities to make meaningful differences, and the wholehearted devotion to those I love, work with, and care for. I believe that every human being has unique gifts and abilities they can share. By learning and applying the 5 Practices of the Caring Mentor, we will strengthen our mentoring relationships from the inside out. We will help our mentees uncover their own talents and maximize their abilities to bring out the best in their students.

INTRODUCTION

As a school counseling specialist for a large urban school district, I often facilitate professional development. One of the most important aspects of this role is to pair new counselors with experienced counselors who will serve as their mentors. When I meet with both new and experienced counselors to begin the mentoring process, I always make it a point to arrive early and greet each person warmly. I ask questions about their lives and truly listen to the answers. The veteran counselors return my affection and interest with understanding and appreciation. The new counselors, however, usually offer a half smile, thinking, *What is this guy doing?*

I like to begin our meetings by acknowledging that some of the participants are probably wondering, *What's with all of the individual greetings and questions?* I then ask, "How many people are busy?" Inevitably, I hear some chuckles, and most of the people in the room raise their hands. Next, I ask the group to raise their hands if a typical day leaves them feeling rushed, as if they are running from one task to the next, always trying to catch up but never quite making it. Again, I'm answered by a wave of laughter and a sea of raised hands. Lastly, I ask the participants to raise their hands if they feel stressed and overwhelmed as a result of having a daily to-do list that requires more time to complete than there are hours in the day. Sure enough, murmurs filter through the crowd, and people nod at one another in recognition.

By now, the anxiety that had been hidden under the surface becomes palpable, and the group acknowledges that in a world where technology and communication move faster than we do, we are all feeling the pressure. I explain that we live in a fast-paced environment in which it's easy to get straight to business with people and immediately place our focus on procedures, data, accountability, standards, evaluations, and measurable results. In this mode of being, however, we forget the importance of our human connections with one another.

In the rush to survive the day, we become functionaries rather than real people with thoughts and feelings that matter, and we lose sight of why we're doing what we're doing in the first place.

To emphasize this point, I tell the group that my greetings are a way to express that I'm glad to see them. They represent my commitment to putting our human connections first in our mentoring relationships.

Next, I invite everyone to greet at least three other people with warmth, encouraging them to take genuine interest in their colleagues by asking questions about their lives. I ask them not just to say the words but to ask their questions with sincerity, to be curious, to want to know how the other person is doing, and then to listen with all of their attention—not just with their ears but with all their senses—truly hearing, seeing, and feeling the person with the fullness of their presence.

People always come to life during these exchanges. Their faces light up with authentic smiles, they laugh naturally, and they fill the room with openness, goodwill, and well-being. In fact, it usually takes a few minutes to bring the group back together because everyone is so wholeheartedly engaged. Afterward, I question the counselors about their experience and answers pour out. Here are some typical responses I receive:

"It felt wonderful to give my full attention to another person."

"It was healing just to be listened to."

"I had forgotten how important it is to stop everything and just talk with each other."

"I feel nourished and connected with myself and the group."

Having created an environment of attentiveness and mutual care, we are now ready to talk about mentoring.

Why do these genuine interactions have such a powerful effect? In my view, it's because people are naturally inclined to care. Although we are often exposed to reports of cruelty, I've witnessed firsthand how people care for one another in the wake of tragic events. Whether it is expressed through parents loving their children, neighbors reaching out after the devastation of a hurricane, or the large numbers of people who volunteer to assist others throughout the world, care is at the heart of who we are as human beings, even though the intensity of life may tend to bury it.

What Is Mentoring?

Mentoring refers to a supportive relationship in which a more knowledgeable, and experienced person educates, counsels, encourages, and guides a less knowledgeable and experienced person in order to enhance professional or personal growth. Teacher and school counselor mentors are experienced educators who support less experienced teachers and school counselors.

These mentors help their mentees navigate their first years in the profession while discovering their strengths and developing their knowledge and skills. They also assist their mentees as they learn to meet challenges, become contributing members of the school community, and work with students effectively.

At times, this work takes place within the context of formal mentoring as part of an organized program, while at other times it may be a more informal relationship outside of an organized program.

What Does It Mean to Care within the Mentoring Role?

I've learned through many years of study, research, and practice that the key ingredient to an effective mentoring relationship, whether it is formal or informal, is care. Care refers to the compassionate concern and action that occurs within a relationship, characterized by engagement, connection, and sensitivity to the mentee's needs. Merriam-Webster's dictionary defines *caring* as "feeling or showing concern for or kindness to others." The word comes from the Old English term *carian* or *cearn*, which means "to be anxious or solicitous; to grieve; to feel concern or interest."

Caring for others means that their well-being matters deeply to us. We feel other people's pain, unease, or discomfort, and we seek to alleviate it through compassionate action. We also recognize the capacity of others for happiness and seek to support the realization of their full potential. Care requires a desire to know and understand other human beings, to be sensitive to and responsive to their needs, and to be committed to their ongoing growth. This takes place through relationships based upon respect, empathy, generosity, helpfulness, and authentic human connection.

It's important to emphasize here that expressing care in a mentoring relationship is different than enabling. Care focuses on meeting the needs of mentees while also empowering them to learn to meet their own needs. Enabling, on the other hand, occurs when mentors do things for mentees that they could do for themselves. It precludes taking the needed actions to help them grow and develop the ability to stand on their own two feet.

Care is not a form of self-sacrifice and doesn't require mentors to ignore their own needs. In fact, caring mentors make self-care a priority (chapter 8 of this book is devoted to self-care), set healthy boundaries, and honor their own needs while remaining focused on assisting mentees as they develop their professional autonomy.

The Benefits of Being a Caring Mentor

Being a caring mentor has been the single most rewarding aspect of my professional life. Each time I apply the practices in this book, I feel a strong sense of personal satisfaction knowing I'm giving the fullness of my heart to my mentees, not just to help them succeed professionally but also to support their growth and wellness as human beings. It's also gratifying to know that implementing the 5 Practices of the Caring Mentor not only helps my mentees but also has a positive impact on each and every student with whom they will work.

In addition to the joy I've received from watching mentees and their students thrive, serving as a caring mentor has helped me to grow as a caring person and develop my own mentoring skills, as well as build meaningful and productive relationships. Being a mentor has been a deeply fulfilling way of passing my knowledge and experience along to the next generation of educators.

My work as a caring mentor has also taken me to the next level in my career. After establishing myself as an experienced counselor at the school level, I became aware of an influx of new school counselors to our district. Recognizing the value I could bring to this group through caring mentorships, I volunteered to meet with new counselors both individually and in small groups throughout the year. Soon, the new counselors began to thrive at their schools.

As the director and other leaders from our county's school counseling department observed the positive effects of my work mentoring the new counselors, they offered me a position as a school counseling specialist at the district level. As a result of this promotion, I'm now in my fourth year as a district leader. I love the work I do every day, and I'm grateful for the opportunity to influence other educators on a larger scale.

Understanding the role of care and developing the ability to express care effectively both help mentoring relationships thrive. A successful mentorship has many valuable outcomes. For the individual, serving as a caring mentor can bring personal satisfaction, professional growth, and opportunities for career advancement. Schools and school districts also benefit from caring mentorships, which result in increased educator retention and enhanced performance from teachers and school counselors, in turn leading to improved student achievement.

This Book's Intended Audience

This book is intended for teacher and school counselor mentors, instructional coaches, school administrators and principals, district leaders, and those who coordinate or oversee educational mentoring programs. It was also written for anyone who wants to better understand the role of caring in mentoring relationships within the educational setting, as well as those who want to learn powerful practices designed to express care in ways that bring out the best in teacher and school counselor mentees.

The practices shared within these pages will serve educational mentors and anyone overseeing mentoring programs for any grade level from prekindergarten to 12th grade. It is designed to support mentors at all levels of experience. The practices outlined here apply equally well to both teacher and school counselor mentoring relationships.

The Problems Mentors Face and the Caring Solution

My doctoral dissertation indicated that caring practices have a profound positive impact on educational mentoring relationships, and that there is a need for increased focus and training in this area. From my research and experience, there are many problems mentors face when trying to infuse their mentoring relationships with care. Frequently, mentors experience high levels of stress as a result of overwhelming workloads, unending paperwork, and other pressing demands, making it difficult to strike a balance between the time needed to engage in meaningful mentoring and their other work responsibilities.

Most studies agree that new educators experience a multitude of challenges as they seek to navigate their first years as a teacher or school counselor. From a leadership perspective, district administrators, mentoring coordinators, and school principals seek solutions to the challenge of retaining teachers and school counselors while also supporting them in their work with students. The National Center for Education Statistics reported that educator attrition is a major issue, and while further research is needed, several studies show that effective mentoring contributes to teacher retention.

The 5 Practices of the Caring Mentor provides solutions to these challenges. As new educators work with mentors who have the knowledge and skills to care effectively, they receive the support needed to overcome the inevitable difficulties of their first years in the profession, increasing the likelihood of building a successful career and enhancing their abilities to contribute toward students' academic attainment, social-emotional growth, and life readiness.

Conversely, I've seen time and again that when mentoring relationships are not built upon a solid foundation of care, mentors and mentees often lose trust. Their time together becomes less productive, their job performance and satisfaction decline, and eventually they experience burnout. The 5 Practices of the Caring Mentor are much more than feel-good ideas or an extra set of tasks to add to an already packed schedule. The information in this book has the potential to transform mentoring relationships into powerfully caring experiences that lead to reduced stress, meaningful teaching and learning, emotional support, and deep satisfaction for both mentors and their mentees, who find they are growing, thriving, and contributing meaningfully to their professions.

What You Will Learn from This Book

The majority of books and articles I've encountered emphasize the technical aspects of mentoring, including goal setting, timelines, corrective feedback, and other methodological skills. While those objectives are important, this book is different because it focuses on an approach to mentoring centered on care, which I find is the single most important factor in building and sustaining successful mentoring relationships. This book will help teacher and school counselor mentors put the humanity of their mentees first by learning evidence-based practices for infusing their mentoring relationships with care.

In our fast-paced, results-oriented, and often stressful world, this is far from easy. As we journey together through these chapters, I share research gleaned from both my dissertation and interviews with current teachers, school counselors, and mentors. I also share stories and insights gained from my experiences as a mentor and a mentee. In addition, I provide tools and exercises to help you apply the practices successfully, some of which are easy, while others require more time and effort.

Through this book, you'll discover ways to forge an authentic connection with your mentees, allowing you to work together not only mind to mind but also heart to heart. You'll learn to infuse your mentoring relationships with emotional safety, and you'll discover methods to support your mentees' ongoing growth. In addition, you'll develop powerful ways to share your experiences and perspectives while assisting your mentees in clarifying and learning from their own. You'll discover the value of taking concrete actions to support your mentees' success, and, finally, you'll learn a caring approach to concluding your mentoring relationships meaningfully, helpfully, and harmoniously.

Composites and Privacy

The mentors and mentees described within these pages represent real people. Some, however, are composites that I've created to convey the concepts in this book. In these cases, the events are true, but sometimes work that took place within different mentoring relationships is combined into a single narrative to provide a more succinct presentation of the practices. The dialogue is not given verbatim, but it captures the general essence and truth of what was expressed. I've also changed the names, locations, and other identifying details within the stories to protect the privacy of the participants.

What You Will Find in Each Chapter

In the following chapters, I provide key insights and strategies to empower your mentoring success by sharing the 5 Practices of the Caring Mentor. These practices are as follows:

- Caring Mentor Practice #1: Caring mentors practice active listening to make a sincere connection with their mentees.

- Caring Mentor Practice #2: Caring mentors create a safe place for authentic expression.

- Caring Mentor Practice #3: Caring mentors devote themselves to their mentees' growth.

- Caring Mentor Practice #4: Caring mentors share their perspectives and insights with their mentees.

- Caring Mentor Practice #5: Caring mentors act on behalf of their mentees.

Chapter 1 discusses the importance of mentors practicing active listening to make a sincere connection with their mentees and enhance their well-being and professional success. Chapter 2 focuses on the need for mentors to create a safe place for their mentees to be themselves and express their thoughts and feelings openly. Chapter 3 deals with guiding mentors as they devote themselves to their mentees' ongoing growth and development. Chapter 4 outlines methods mentors can use to share perspectives and helpful insights with their mentees. Chapter 5 delves into the value of mentors taking concrete actions on behalf of their mentees. Chapter 6 provides strategies for when mentees resist the mentoring process. Chapter 7 examines caring ways to work with mentees during times of crisis, and chapter 8 emphasizes the importance of self-care and how to honor your own needs as a mentor. In the conclusion, I provide strategies for bringing mentorships to a positive and productive close, highlighting the unconditional love, respect, and kindness that form the foundation of caring mentoring.

Let's Get Started

Just as I do at our district mentoring meetings, I've set the stage here for our work together. During this journey, I discuss the specific practices needed to care effectively as I equip you to become a mentor who brings out the best in your mentees. I now invite you to explore the 5 Practices of the Caring Mentor with me so you can strengthen your mentoring relationships from the inside out.

CHAPTER 1

Caring Mentor Practice #1

Caring Mentors Practice Active Listening to Make a Sincere
Connection with Their Mentees

S erving as a caring mentor is much more than making sure our mentees are producing tangible results. To truly help our mentees thrive, we need to get to know them personally and show them we are not only invested in their professional achievement, but we care about them as individuals. In this chapter, we explore the importance of practicing active listening and discuss key strategies that form the basis of our caring mentoring relationships, including honoring our mentees' stories, sharing our own stories, and helping our mentees discover and express their gifts.

Listen Actively and Make a Connection with Your Mentee

I met Mr. Carson for the first time when I interviewed for a school counselor position at the inner-city elementary school where he served as principal. A tall man, he wore an elegant shirt and tie with his hair swept over his head in a perfect wave. He looked like a father from a 1950's sitcom. I wiped my sweaty palms on the sides of my pants and entered Mr. Carson's office. The room felt like a cozy den in someone's home, not a principal's office, with its carpeted floor, old wooden desk, and autographed photos of baseball greats from the sixties covering the walls.

When we took our seats for the interview, I expected Mr. Carson to fire off a series of questions, inquiring about my professional qualifications. Instead, he asked me questions about my family, the sports I had played as a kid, and my hometown. Then he shared stories about his mom and dad, his basketball career, and what it was like growing up in western Pennsylvania. I immediately felt connected with Mr. Carson. I could tell he liked and respected me by the way he expressed interest in who I was as a person and the way he shared about himself from the heart.

After a long conversation, Mr. Carson leaned in and said, "Now let me tell you about our students." He talked about how many students were enrolled for kindergarten without ever having opened a book or ever having been exposed to reading of any kind. He shared stories of students' frustrations in the classroom and the difficulties they faced at home. Soon, the interview was no longer about getting the job. My time with Mr. Carson became a candid discussion about my life, the gifts I had to offer his school, and how we could make a difference in the lives of students and their families. In fact, Mr. Carson never asked me a single question about my resume or work credentials.

Right from the start, Mr. Carson made our connection and working relationship a priority. Before long, he was not only my principal but a trusted mentor and friend. As a result, he was able to create the circumstances I needed to grow professionally and succeed in my work with our students. For example, Mr. Carson placed my office in the heart of the school, right next to the front desk. He wanted me to be in the center of things in our building. Everything related to our school community passed through my office, and before long I established the relationships with students, parents, and staff that helped me best meet their needs as a school counselor.

Mr. Carson and I started each school day side by side, sharing positive messages on the morning announcements and getting our students ready to learn. He gave me the time and space to counsel children in crisis and to meet with those who needed help with academic, social, and emotional issues. Under Mr.

Carson's guidance, I facilitated small groups that taught social skills, conflict mediation, and study strategies. I had access to every classroom where I shared lessons in support of the success of both students and teachers.

I ran many school-wide initiatives, such as character education assemblies, anti-bullying campaigns, and events to inspire students to attend college. I worked with our staff and a community church to provide groceries, gift baskets during the holidays, school uniforms, and backpacks filled with supplies to families in need. Mr. Carson also allowed me to bring in tutors, guest readers, and speakers, such as the mayor. In addition, I organized field trips for students to visit city hall and our local university. With Mr. Carson's encouragement and support, I even began mentoring other school counselors from around the district in our school's media center.

At that point in my career, I had been an educator for many years, but through Mr. Carson's caring mentorship I began to come into my own as a person and professional. Mr. Carson's role as my mentor was the foundation for everything I accomplished, and the way in which he took a sincere personal interest in me was the key to my professional growth during that time.

I've often reflected on why Mr. Carson's mentoring inspired me so deeply and contributed so much to my growth. When we see that another person, especially a trusted mentor, is genuinely concerned about our well-being and who we are as a person, we feel more connected and give our best to both the mentoring relationship and our professional practice.

Another question I've asked myself is, *How did Mr. Carson express his caring support in a way that I could receive it effectively?* First and foremost, Mr. Carson always took the time to listen. Whenever we spoke, he treated me as if I were the most important person he knew. Even though Mr. Carson was usually busy in his own role as principal, he always found time to work with me.

I was also struck by Mr. Carson's authentic curiosity. He was never overbearing, meddlesome, or intrusive when he asked questions. Instead, he asked them because he truly wanted to get to know me. In fact, he frequently started conversations by asking about my family or my activities outside of school rather than jumping straight to business. Mr. Carson made our personal connection the first priority, and that bond translated into a strong working relationship. When Mr. Carson listened to me, he understood me, which gave him valuable insight about how to best relate to me, collaborate effectively, and be of service to my personal and professional development.

Be Authentic and Develop Cultural Competence

I met with Yvette, a first-grade teacher in her sixth year, on a cool Saturday morning at a local café. We sat in a quiet corner and, over coffee, I asked her about her experiences being mentored during her first year. Between sips, Yvette shared that her mentor Dr. Evans, who was a veteran educator at the time, cared for her authentically. Yvette described how Dr. Evans's genuine concern helped her to thrive as she began her career. During her first year of teaching, Yvette had been working through some difficulties in her personal life. Dr. Evans, however, tuned in to her emotions, according to Yvette, "like a mother." Yvette continued, "If I was struggling at home, she could see it on my face and she'd talk with me and help me through it."

I was curious what approach Dr. Evans took to help Yvette with her emotional struggles, and I asked her to tell me more. Yvette shared that Dr. Evans often visited her classroom after school to check in and see how Yvette was doing. During these visits, Dr. Evans asked Yvette how things were going at home and at school. Yvette pointed out that Dr. Evans was not asking these questions "just to be polite," but because she wanted to understand what it was Yvette was going through.

As the server refilled our coffee, Yvette told me Dr. Evans's authentic interest in her as a person and her willingness to listen helped Yvette express her feelings rather than hold them in. This allowed Dr. Evans to get to know Yvette on a deeper level, not only as a teacher but also as a human being. Yvette rested her chin on her hand and said, "The first year of teaching is hard, and I had challenges outside of school. Dr. Evans understood that and was there to help me. She didn't just care about teaching and lesson plans, she cared about my happiness too."

Yvette went on to share how she appreciated the interest Dr. Evans took in her Haitian American heritage. She said, "We were from different cultures, but Dr. Evans always wanted to learn more about that." For example, when Dr. Evans asked about Yvette's life growing up, Yvette explained how her parents taught her not to sustain eye contact and how sometimes in her culture it takes extra time to build trust. Additionally, Yvette related how Dr. Evans took the time to learn some words and phrases in Haitian-Creole. Those efforts, Yvette explained, made her feel respected. Her conversations with Dr. Evans led them to explore children's literature written by Haitian American authors, which eventually translated into rich cultural lessons for both their students.

That afternoon, as I reviewed my notes from my conversation with Yvette, I reflected on how the ability of mentors to get to know their mentees is directly connected to the mentee's feeling of being cared for. Authenticity is key because mentees can sense false care, when their mentors simply go through the motions of asking questions instead of expressing genuine concern. In fact, pretending to care can be damaging to the mentoring relationship because it breaks the vital trust needed for successful mentoring relationships to flourish.

Dr. Evans's regular check-ins provided Yvette with consistent support. This let Yvette know that she was not alone, plus it gave her the opportunity to ask questions and express concerns. The respect with which Dr. Evans treated Yvette established the trusting bond mentoring relationships need to thrive. To accomplish the same with my mentees, I set an ongoing reminder on my cell phone to check in with them at the same time each week. The purpose of these calls is to stay in touch and offer general support rather than to accomplish any specific goal. My mentees have shared with me that these check-ins were a source of ongoing comfort and a valuable opportunity to discuss progress or seek guidance.

In addition to their regular check-ins, Yvette appreciated that Dr. Evans viewed her as a whole person rather than solely as a mentee or just another teacher with whom she was working. When Dr. Evans showed compassion for Yvette's personal struggles and life outside of school, she strengthened their relationship, supported Yvette's well-being, and mitigated some of the effects these challenges may have had upon her work.

I was struck by the way in which Dr. Evans supported Yvette through learning about her Haitian American background. This element of their relationship allowed Yvette to open up about herself and her heritage, and it helped Dr. Evans to better understand Yvette as a person and a professional. Exploring Haitian culture also gave Yvette an opportunity to take on a teaching role within the mentoring relationship, showing Dr. Evans another side of her personality.

Of course, it is important that mentors do not impose on mentees in any way or interrogate them with too many questions. This may make the mentee feel as if the mentor is prying. Inquiries about a mentee's culture should be gentle, nonthreatening, and stem from a sincere curiosity to better know the mentee. When mentors take the time to learn about their mentees' cultures, it deepens the mentoring relationship and honors the mentee as a person.

Discover and Honor Your Mentees' Strengths

In my work coaching mentors, I've noticed a trend of starting mentoring interactions by focusing on mentees' problems. This is a natural course of action. When mentors see mentees struggling, their first inclination is usually to identify the challenges and work toward solutions. It is often more effective, however, to begin by determining mentees' strengths and helping them explore and express those strengths in their work.

When I sit down with my mentees, one of my first goals is to take note of their good qualities and to explore what motivates them to give their best. New and experienced educators alike are frequently struggling, but when I listen with the intention to discover my mentees' unique strengths, I always find fresh opportunities to support their growth. The following account illustrates this point.

During the course of my mentoring relationship with Simone, a veteran elementary school counselor and devoted mother, I noticed shifts in her level of motivation as we discussed her work. Over the course of multiple conversations, I sensed she'd become less enthused with the counseling activities she had once been excited about. I had known Simone for years, and she was usually one of our most enthusiastic counselors, so this trend concerned me. As I had learned from Mr. Carson, caring for Simone needed to take the form of asking her questions about how she was feeling, not just about her career but her life as a whole.

To better explore what was happening with Simone, I suggested we meet weekly. One afternoon over lunch, Simone shared how she'd watched her children struggle with identifying and pursuing post-secondary options. In the process of researching ways to assist her family, she had developed an interest in becoming a high school counselor. When I asked Simone to tell me more about what she was learning, her eyes lit up, and she shared her passion for helping students gain access to college and the career opportunities that followed.

Together, we discovered that supporting secondary students was not just a passing interest but a deep calling. Taking the time to get to know Simone as a human being rather than focusing solely on our agenda for the day allowed me to understand her on a deeper level and recognize the untapped strength and passion she possessed.

As we honored Simone's feelings, giving them time to emerge naturally in our conversations, she realized the time had come to start a second career as a counselor at the high school level. Discovering and acting upon this fresh purpose gave Simone renewed energy and motivation, and she is now "excited again" in her role working with older students.

As caring mentors, we have to let go of our own preconceived ideas about what is best for our mentees and instead allow our work to be guided by the understanding that only comes from deep listening over the course of time. For mentors to be truly helpful, we need to invest our energy in understanding our mentees' motivations, talents, and deeper aspirations. This often requires us to get to know our mentees on a personal level.

This is not to say that we should treat mentees as friends with no professional boundaries. However, while these relationships have a professional focus, they should also contain the sense of warmth and concern that occurs within friendships. This quality lets the mentee know we genuinely care, plus it opens the door to the mutual vulnerability required for impactful conversations.

After establishing a connection with Simone, I was able to gain a clearer understanding of how she was really feeling. "When did you first start feeling a pull toward working with older students? What did it feel like? How would an ideal day of school counseling look for you at the secondary level? What do you really want?" These are examples of the questions I explored with Simone.

Mentoring Simone taught me that effective listening means listening with a purpose. This purpose is to express care and to connect with mentees in an attempt to understand their experiences and perspectives. Simone's responses hinted at the struggles she was experiencing in her current role and the powerful enthusiasm she had for working with students at the secondary level. This understanding in turn led to a series of candid conversations that helped Simone take the next step in her professional development, a step that improved her ability to help students while also creating an opportunity for a school counselor who was ready to step into the position at the elementary level.

Strengths assessments are another method of helping mentees discover and understand their strengths. Although mentees often believe they already know themselves well, the results of these assessments provide fresh insights into their personal assets, values, and passions. I list three such assessments in the Suggested Reading and Resources section at the end of this book.

The Caring Mentor Active Listening Exercises

A common theme in each of the stories in this chapter is that expressing care through a sincere personal interest in your mentee requires active listening. To be an active listener, the mentor must be fully present and put everything else aside, ready to devote his or her whole heart and mind to whatever the mentee is saying. Active listening includes open and welcoming body language, checking for understanding, asking good questions, receiving information respectfully and without judgment, and, when possible, empowering mentees to discover their own solutions to their challenges. In the following sections, I share several of the active listening exercises I use when training mentors to listen effectively.

Mindfulness Meditation

Mindfulness meditation provides mentors with a way to practice being present with their mentees and to develop the capacity to bring their attention back to what the mentee is saying whenever the mind wanders. When I guide participants through this exercise, I begin with a few deep, relaxing breaths. Then I lead participants through a scan of their body, asking them to bring awareness to each part systematically, beginning with the top of the head before moving to the face, back of the head, neck, shoulders, arms, chest, stomach, etc., all the way to

27

the soles of their feet. This practice helps mentors center their attention in the present moment.

Next, I instruct mentors to become conscious of their breathing, first following the breath in until they reach full inhalation, then noticing the pause between breaths, and finally following their breath all the way out. Participants continue to follow their breathing in this manner for several minutes, paying attention to when the mind drifts off into thoughts of the past or future, then gently bringing their attention back to the present breath. After that, I ask participants to notice how their thoughts and feelings come and go while maintaining their awareness. I encourage them to stay centered as the observer of their experiences. Lastly, I bring participants' attention back to their breathing and invite them to slowly return and engage with the group.

Mindfulness is a key practice for mentors because it is easy to become distracted during mentoring conversations. In many cases, our minds wander or something our mentee says triggers an inner dialogue that pulls our attention away from the current situation and toward our own thoughts and feelings. Developing the ability to notice when our minds drift and to return to full engagement allows us to stay focused and puts us in a stronger position to mentor effectively.

Body Language and Reflecting Thoughts and Feelings

After the body scan and several minutes of mindful breathing, the group pairs off and I review the basics of listening with the mentors. These include sitting up comfortably but relatively straight, leaning slightly forward to show interest, making gentle eye contact, nodding periodically to indicate understanding, and maintaining open facial expressions.

Next, I ask one of the mentors in each pair to speak about his or her morning. The other partner practices listening, paying attention to the speaker's content while identifying the emotions behind the words. After one minute, I ask the listeners to reflect back to the speaker what he or she said and to gently inquire about the emotions they sensed behind the words.

The speakers then give the listeners feedback about the accuracy of their reflections and sense of the speakers' feelings. After this exchange is complete, the partners switch roles.

Open-Ended Questions

For the next activity, I ask each speaker to talk about a hobby or favorite pastime while their partner listens closely and asks questions about the topic. For example, if the speaker says she enjoys volleyball, the listener might ask, "How did you first become interested in volleyball? What position do you play? What is it that you like most about volleyball? What advice would you have for a beginner who wants to learn to play?"

I encourage the speakers and listeners to respond to one another as they give and receive information, forming a type of verbal dance. I usually give the participants three to five minutes for these exchanges before they switch roles. Asking questions in this way shows sincere interest, builds trust, and helps each mentor learn more about their "mentee," allowing them to provide more effective support.

Guided Problem-Solving

To begin this activity, I ask each speaker to share a small problem with the listener. For the purpose of this exercise, the problem should be a minor one, not something overly heavy or serious. As the speakers share their problems, the listeners ask questions in an effort to explore solutions.

The idea is for the listener (the mentor) to work on the art of believing that the speaker (the mentee) has the ability to solve problems and identify the next positive step forward. The listeners must therefore practice bringing out the mentees' natural wisdom through helpful questions instead of trying to solve the problem themselves.

After three to five minutes, the speakers give the listeners feedback about the effectiveness of their questions and what insights or solutions they gleaned from the exchange. Then the partners switch roles.

Develop Active Listening through Skill Isolation

Skill isolation exercises also help mentors-in-training improve their active listening skills. I developed these exercises as a way to practice receiving the thoughts and emotions of mentees by focusing on one specific aspect of active listening at a time. As mentors work through the following exercises, they learn they must engage many different parts of themselves in order to actively listen and express care to their mentees. They also gain valuable insight into the effectiveness of their efforts by receiving feedback from a partner.

Active Listening through Silence

To practice active listening, I explain to participants that their partner will speak for one minute about a small challenge they encountered that week. When I start the clock, the listeners should focus on listening deeply without speaking or making sounds of any kind. Their concern for their partner should only be expressed through eye contact, facial expressions, and posture. Again, I instruct the participants to switch roles at the end of the exercise.

After each partner has taken a turn, I encourage each participant to share which of their partner's specific actions or silent expressions helped them feel received and accepted. This exercise shows mentors that care is expressed not only in words but also in silence and the way they carry themselves while listening. Often it is the quality of our body language, our presence, and our attention that has the greatest impact.

Active Listening through Speaking

For this exercise, I ask the mentors to sit back-to-back so they cannot see one another. As their partner speaks for one minute about a difficult experience with a student, each mentor is to listen and express caring support using only spoken words. This allows mentors to focus on the words they choose and experiment with how they convey compassion solely through tone of voice and the content of their verbal responses.

Once each partner has had a turn to speak, they give one another feedback about which words and verbal tones most effectively offered support and encouragement. This exercise allows mentors to concentrate on their choice of words and the inflections they use to convey meaning. The feedback they receive helps them learn which word choices and tones of voice are most effective in expressing care.

Active Listening through Text

Next, I ask the pairs of mentors to go to opposite sides of the room, each facing the wall so they cannot see or hear one another. This time, the participants communicate only by texting one another on their cell phones. The "speakers" text their partners with a description of an aspect of their work that makes them feel anxious. The "listeners" then convey their concern by texting their replies. These sessions last five minutes, giving each partner a turn as the "speaker" and the "listener," after which the participants offer feedback about which textual expressions were the most beneficial. This exercise is another way for mentors to practice expressing care solely through word choice, without relying on other means of self-expression.

Listening for Facts, Emotions, Strengths, and Values

To begin this exercise, I ask each participant to write four columns on a piece of paper labeled Facts, Emotions, Strengths, and Values. The pairs sit across from each other again, and while one speaks, I instruct their partner to listen for any facts, emotions, strengths, or values they hear and to write them down in the appropriate columns. Facts are details representing the mentee's perception of truth in a situation, emotions characterize the mentee's felt experience, strengths are gifts the mentee possesses, and values point toward the mentee's strongly held beliefs.

After each partner has had a turn to speak, the participants share their notes and check for accuracy. This helps mentors identify the messages mentees are communicating, both verbally and nonverbally. It also demonstrates how several types of information are conveyed in mentoring conversations and how each type helps mentors get to know and serve their mentees.

Reflection Period

After we complete this series of exercises, I give mentors several minutes to write down their thoughts about how these experiences will impact their mentoring work. I then ask participants to share their observations with the group. Providing time for reflection helps mentors process the experience of practicing these techniques, as well as clarify their thoughts about the value of active listening and each of the different modes of expressing care.

Intentionally practicing the basic skills of mindfulness, reflecting thoughts and feelings, asking questions, guiding mentees toward solutions, and isolating each aspect of communication all help mentees become better active listeners. Mentors report these training exercises prevent them from becoming distracted in mentoring sessions and assist them in refocusing their minds when needed, equipping them to build meaningful connections with their mentees. In my experience, developing these skills reduces misunderstandings, encourages sharing, and puts mentors in a stronger position to empower their mentees.

Suggestions for Practicing Active Listening

The following list outlines specific suggestions for applying Caring Mentor Practice #1 in the areas of developing and applying your active listening skills, being authentic and developing cultural competence, discovering and honoring your mentees' strengths, and cultivating your active listening skills through concentrated practice.

Develop and Apply Your Active Listening Skills

- Get in touch with your natural curiosity about who your mentees are as people and professionals, including their personal stories and future aspirations.

- Make connecting with your mentees a top priority, setting everything else aside as you listen with your full attention—not only to the words but to the emotion and meaning behind the words.

- Offer warm and welcoming body language, which may include making respectful eye contact, smiling to show acceptance, nodding in recognition, and maintaining a relaxed and open posture.

- Ask open-ended questions to show your interest and to know your mentees better.

- Reflect back what your mentees have said to ensure you understand and to let them know they are truly being heard.

Be Authentic and Develop Cultural Competence

- Offer your sincere support during difficult times.

- Share your honest thoughts and feelings while maintaining boundaries and professionalism.

- Set cell phone reminders or mark regular dates on your calendar to check in with your mentees, either through personal visits or with phone calls, texts, emails, or hand-written notes. Remember that building an authentic mentoring relationship is a process that requires time and consistent communication.

- Develop cultural competence by reading about your mentees' cultures, asking respectful questions, and applying what you learn.

Discover and Honor Your Mentees' Strengths

- Learn what motivates and inspires your mentees by asking thoughtful questions.

- Have your mentees write out a list of their strengths.

- Help your mentees explore ways to express their strengths and incorporate them into their work.

- Use strengths assessment tools and discuss the results.

Cultivate Your Active Listening Skills through Practice

- Develop mindfulness by practicing conscious breathing and relaxation techniques.

- Practice the fundamentals of listening, including maintaining open body language, asking open-ended questions, and checking for understanding.

- Recognize the moments when you become distracted and learn to shift your attention back to the practice of active listening.

- Empower your mentees to discover their own solutions to problems.

- Reflect on the importance of active listening and practice the skill isolation exercises in this chapter to develop your own active listening skills.

Bringing It All Together

Caring mentors build meaningful connections with their mentees by listening actively and becoming better acquainted with their mentees both personally and professionally. They make their relationships with their mentees the first priority and demonstrate their care by how they listen and relate. As we learn more about our mentees, we strengthen our professional bonds, increase our understanding of their needs, and discover their passions, strengths, and values, allowing us to better support their success. Now that we have explored the importance of developing a sincere connection with our mentees, it's time to dive into Caring Mentor Practice #2, which focuses on creating a safe place for mentees' authentic expression.

CHAPTER 2

Caring Mentor Practice #2

Caring Mentors Create a Safe Place

for Authentic Expression

F or mentees to truly benefit from mentoring relationships, they need to know they are free to be themselves so they may express their concerns and ask challenging questions. In this chapter, we explore how to create a safe place for mentees by establishing trust, being available and reliable, validating feelings, maintaining confidentiality, applying adult learning principles, and providing mentees with ongoing encouragement.

Establish Trust with Your Mentees

At the beginning of the school year, I meet with each of our district's new school counselors. When I do, I begin by emphasizing that our relationships must be based on trust. I make it clear my intention is not to judge, but to support mentees by encouraging their professional growth. To lighten the mood, I share how during my first year in the profession my main objective during the district office's school visits was to stay out of trouble.

I usually get a good laugh at this. I explain I wasn't sure what I needed to do as a new counselor, much less how to do it. At the time, my primary concern was to make it through my first year without my supervisors viewing me as incompetent. I want my mentees to understand this attitude wasn't helpful for my growth as a school counselor and that as mentors our sole focus is to support our mentees' learning and success.

I always make a point to share this information in a warm and friendly manner, and most of the time my mentees breathe a sigh of relief. Mentoring is a service position. It's an opportunity to give of yourself in a way that benefits others. Setting a positive tone goes a long way toward helping mentees relax and be themselves within their mentoring relationships. As a mentor, however, you can't stop with friendly words. Trust must be earned by putting care into practice.

For example, one of the assignments I give my mentees is to conduct a data analysis and needs assessment at their school. After I teach them this process, I give them several days to complete their assessment, checking in on them periodically to discuss the information they've gathered.

Frank, an older gentleman with tousled gray hair, had just started as a school counselor in our district after many years in a private counseling practice. A few days after I had given him the assignment, he called me to confide that not only was he having trouble with the data and needs assessments, but that he didn't know the username and password he needed to log in to the required system. Frank was embarrassed to share his difficulties, but I helped him gladly, relating that I had gone through similar challenges in my first years as a school counselor.

When I visited Frank at his school, he gave me a hearty double handshake and shared that he usually wouldn't have reached out with that kind of vulnerability in a professional setting before really getting to know someone. My initial talk about trust, however, gave him the confidence to tell me the truth. We sat down at a small table in his office, reviewed the data analysis and needs assessment step-by-step, and then logged in to the system to work on it together.

Knowing Frank needed extra assistance navigating the new system, I encouraged him to ask questions, which I answered with patience and kindness. He completed the task successfully and used the data to provide the needed services to his students. In addition, he learned firsthand I was someone he could trust, and since then, Frank has been open and honest with me throughout our mentoring relationship.

Years of mentoring have taught me mentees need to know they can be completely honest with their mentors in order to truly benefit from the mentoring process. The trust needed to establish and maintain free-flowing and productive communication requires mentors to have a nonjudgmental attitude, express genuine humility, and communicate with transparency and consistency.

As I did with Frank, when I start a new mentoring relationship with a teacher or school counselor, my first priority is to create a safe environment in which my mentees are free to express themselves authentically. I sit with them face-to-face, without a notepad or anything else that might appear formal, and let them know that our time together is about their needs rather than mine. As we've discussed, I ask open-ended questions to get to know my mentees better. I listen with sincere warmth and a nonjudgmental attitude and share parts of my own journey as an educator—especially the mistakes I made and what I learned from them.

I also share my passion for ongoing learning. I make sure they know that although they naturally view me as a teacher, which is a key part of the mentoring role, we are in this together. We are all striving for a purpose greater than ourselves, which is to become the best professionals we can be in order to serve our students and school communities. Although I respect my own knowledge and take on a clear leadership role for my mentees, when I model a dedication to my own professional development and show through my actions what it means to be a lifelong learner, it inspires my mentees to do the same.

Be Available and Dependable, and Maintain Confidentiality

I met with Victoria, a middle school art teacher fresh out of graduate school, in her classroom. As we sat at one of her large, circular work tables, surrounded by the beautiful paintings and sculptures her students had created, she shared how Ms. Johnson, her mentor and a veteran music teacher, made her classroom a safe haven after school.

Victoria looked over the top of her round glasses, smiling appreciatively, and related how Ms. Johnson instructed her to come see her anytime if she had questions or concerns. Ms. Johnson told her, "You're safe here. Your words are safe here. Our conversations are staying between us and are not going anywhere else. I'm going to help you through this."

As Victoria spoke, the earnestness in her voice showed how touched she was by the sense of safety she experienced with Ms. Johnson. I asked her, "How did it feel when Ms. Johnson made a point to build trust with you, and what other things did she do to help you feel safe?"

Victoria pushed her long, straight hair behind her ear and described the sense of comfort she felt with Ms. Johnson and how she appreciated the way in which Ms. Johnson protected their "talking space." Victoria explained that if another person entered the room while they were speaking, Ms. Johnson would handle the matter quickly and then return to their conversation rather than inviting the other person in during a vulnerable moment. "She never talked about confidential things in front of someone else; it was just me and her when I needed to talk."

Ms. Johnson also provided her cell phone number. "If I felt the need to call her," Victoria said, "even at night, I knew I could. Even if I didn't call, the feeling that I could if I needed to was very important to me. It made me feel that I was always supported." Ms. Johnson also responded to texts and emails promptly, which kept the lines of communication open and let Victoria know that it was okay to reach out.

Clearly Ms. Johnson's availability was one of the most important factors in her mentoring relationship with Victoria. Their mentoring sessions did not always need to be formal arrangements. Ms. Johnson's welcoming attitude made Victoria feel comfortable and less alone at school. It also put Victoria at ease when she needed to talk with Ms. Johnson, which resulted in more frequent meetings and more opportunities for learning and support.

Victoria also appreciated that her interactions with Ms. Johnson remained confidential. This allowed her to speak freely and trust that her words would not be shared with anyone else without her permission. Victoria also knew that the extent to which she opened up was her decision, another key element of their relationship. In other words, while Ms. Johnson was available for Victoria, she made it clear that Victoria was not obligated to share any personal information unless she felt it was appropriate and helpful. Mentors should always, however, make mentees aware of the limits of confidentiality. If a mentee were to disclose information about hurting himself or herself or others, the mentor would be obligated to report it.

Another way Ms. Johnson expressed her care for Victoria was by making their mentoring relationship a priority. Of course, it is not always possible to be available every moment of the day, but Victoria knew she could depend on Ms. Johnson. Victoria said when Ms. Johnson made a promise that she kept it, and that she was willing to put other matters aside to work with Victoria when needed. Ms. Johnson's prompt responses to Victoria's texts, emails, and phone calls contributed to their bond of trust, showing Victoria she could fully rely on Ms. Johnson. Because Ms. Johnson made being available a priority and committed to keeping their conversations confidential, Victoria felt safe enough to share her vulnerabilities and receive the support she needed from the mentoring relationship.

Validate Your Mentees' Feelings

Charlotte, a passionate school counselor in her early twenties, called me to discuss a personality clash she was having with one of the administrators at her school. She shared how this administrator, in her words, "was always putting me down and not letting me do my job." Knowing how heated things had been between her and the administrator, I asked Charlotte how she had responded in those situations. After a pause, she admitted she had been less than respectful to the administrator during some of their exchanges.

Charlotte's difficulties with the administrator resulted in a strained relationship and a tense work environment. This became a distraction for Charlotte, interfering with her best work. I needed to address Charlotte's behavior and make her aware that her inappropriate exchanges with the administrator needed to stop. But Charlotte also needed a safe place to share her thoughts and feelings so I could support her in a real and meaningful way.

I visited Charlotte after school the next day. As we walked the track, I asked how she felt about her relationship with the administrator, and before long, it became clear that her primary emotion was anger. After identifying the core emotion behind the conflict, my next steps were to validate Charlotte's feelings, to empathize with her, and to provide emotional support by listening compassionately as she told me her story.

Although I didn't agree with the way Charlotte had addressed the administrator, I understood her anger and shared that it was important for her to stand up for what she believed in. I also told her about a time when I had lost perspective during a disagreement, letting her know she was not alone in her experience. These exchanges showed Charlotte that I sincerely wanted to support her, and the level of trust they established set the stage for more in-depth work.

Once Charlotte released some of the emotional charge by sharing her story, understanding I empathized with her perspective, we were able to explore the situation more deeply. At that point, I suggested some alternative ways of viewing the situation and working with her feelings.

I asked Charlotte if I could challenge her with what might feel like some difficult questions. She smiled and nodded, and so I asked, "What qualities in the administrator upset you most?" Charlotte said that the administrator had been loud and aggressive. I then asked, "Can you see any of those same qualities in yourself?"

Charlotte took a deep breath, retied her ponytail, and looked at me as if to say, *Are we really going there?* We shared a laugh, and she admitted, "Yes, I'm familiar with those qualities."

I followed up by asking, "What does it mean to you that you and the administrator share these same attributes?"

"It means that I can relate to her," Charlotte said. "It means that I might not like what she's doing, but I can understand it."

Then I prompted Charlotte to share the good qualities she saw in the administrator. She shared that the administrator was passionate and wanted to be great at her job. I asked Charlotte if she could relate to this, and she acknowledged she possessed those qualities as well.

As Charlotte learned to see aspects of herself in the administrator, she was able to relate to the administrator's feelings and find more productive ways to interact with her. Charlotte also discovered this new understanding allowed her to view her relationship with the administrator more objectively, and she could therefore make more helpful decisions about how to work with her.

After our conversation, Charlotte reported that her relationship with the administrator improved and she was better able to focus on her work. She thanked me for "being real" with her. A key point here is that, as mentioned in the previous section, Charlotte and I needed to develop trust before I challenged her to address her emotions on a deeper level. Once Charlotte felt safe with me, she expressed herself honestly, giving us the ability to move toward real solutions.

As part of the process of building trust and establishing a safe place for Charlotte to express herself, it was essential that I validate her feelings. Validation means taking the time to explore, relate to, and accept the other person's emotions. This does not mean that I agreed with Charlotte or that I felt her angry responses to the administrator were appropriate. Instead, it meant I tried to understand the emotions she was experiencing and didn't judge her for the way she was feeling.

Although I knew my work with Charlotte needed to lead to a change in her behavior, I didn't try to fix the way she was feeling. When mentees' feelings are not validated, they often feel rejected, unsupported, and less connected, creating barriers to communication and impeding our ability to mentor effectively. However, when mentors create an atmosphere of emotional safety by validating our mentees' feelings, we build trust and can then explore the deeper issues behind those feelings.

Respect Your Mentees as Equal Adults

As caring mentors, it's important we remember we are working with other adults and that adults have specific learning needs, which are much different from those of children. Adults have their own viewpoints built upon a lifetime of experience. These experiences need to be understood and respected in order to create the safe space required for effective mentoring to occur.

During my first year working at the district level, I was tasked with mentoring Dr. Williams, an accomplished teacher in her early fifties who decided later in her career to become a school counselor. Dr. Williams was well versed in pedagogical methods, had extensive knowledge about the developmental needs of students, and brought a wealth of experience to her new role as a school counselor.

When we began our mentoring relationship, my first priority was to honor Dr. Williams's experiences and achievements by showing respect for the knowledge she had gained during her career. I therefore spent our initial meeting asking questions to learn more about Dr. Williams while listening and expressing appreciation for her professional accomplishments.

Safety in mentoring relationships must be built upon a strong foundation of respect. Once I had a feel for what Dr. Williams already knew, and she felt respected as an accomplished educator, I asked her how I could best help her succeed in her new position. Dr. Williams was familiar with the processes of collaborative planning, data analysis, and needs assessments as she had learned these skills as a teacher. What most interested Dr. Williams was how to work individually with students and how to facilitate small groups.

By first creating a sense of mutual respect and understanding, Dr. Williams felt safe enough to tell me what kinds of mentoring assistance she needed. After we determined she wanted to further develop her approach in leading individual and group sessions with students, I taught her about Brief Solution-Focused Counseling. I also shared the key components of running successful groups, which includes choosing topics, selecting students, scheduling, logistics, curricula, managing behavior, and measurement. By honoring Dr. Williams as a respected professional, we built a mentoring relationship that was not only open and honest but also effective in helping her take the next steps in her professional growth.

My mentoring relationship with Dr. Williams demonstrates that an essential aspect of creating a safe mentoring atmosphere is to honor our mentees as equal adults. Malcom Knowles's adult learning principles provide an excellent foundation for establishing an environment in which mentees are respected for who they are throughout the mentoring process.

Knowles understood adults possess specific characteristics as learners, including a need for their life experiences to be respected, a need for independence, and a need for learning to be relevant to the current circumstances of their lives. By applying these principles throughout the mentoring process, mentees receive a clear message that they are respected and are free to be themselves.

When mentees aren't treated as respected adults or provided with the opportunity to make decisions about their own learning, they become reluctant to participate fully in the process. In this case, they either resist mentoring or settle for compliance rather than authentic engagement. If, as mentors, we do not honor the life experiences of our mentees, then they won't feel seen and heard. Without the opportunity to apply their learning to real-life situations, mentees view the mentoring relationship as another task to be accomplished instead of feeling genuinely motivated to learn and grow.

To apply some of the key principles of adult learning, I suggest setting aside time to become better acquainted with your mentees. These conversations offer an opportunity to learn about mentees' lives, the journey that led them into the field of education, and what it is they hope to accomplish through their work.

I like to think of this process in terms of honoring our mentees' past, present, and future. We honor the past by listening closely to mentees' stories, honor the present by giving our full attention as conversations unfold, and honor the future by helping mentees develop and follow through on plans to achieve their goals. Following these guidelines goes a long way toward establishing the mutual respect needed to create meaningful, relevant, and productive mentoring experiences.

Be Encouraging and See the Best in Your Mentees

Matthew, a retired educator in his midsixties, served as my informal mentor for several years. He showed me a powerful example of what it means to provide a safe place for authentic expression. Matthew made himself available by phone every Thursday evening for many years. During these conversations, we reviewed my week, discussing what went well, where I struggled, and how I could continue to grow as an educator.

Our mentoring relationship, however, was not limited to these weekly meetings.

Matthew also encouraged me to email him every day. This exercise gave me another safe place to express my feelings, share ideas, let my thoughts flow freely, reflect on what I was learning, and consider what I could improve. Matthew made it clear from the beginning that he wouldn't always respond to my emails in writing, although he sometimes did, but he would always read them and respond verbally during our phone conversations.

Writing these emails had the same effect on me as keeping a journal. For many years, I documented my thoughts and feelings and referred to them during difficult times, gaining valuable perspectives. These emails also offered me a secure place to vent my frustrations and reflect on my successes. In addition, they provided Matthew with a glimpse of my daily work and life that wouldn't have been possible without a safe environment in which I could communicate. This, in turn, gave him many key insights to better understand and support me.

What I appreciated most about Matthew as a mentor was that he always saw the good in me and helped me to see the good in myself. He encouraged me to express myself fully, and even if he didn't agree with everything I said or did, he always showed respect for my point of view. Even when I felt down on myself or shared stories about my mistakes, Matthew recognized my positive intentions and directed my focus to what I could learn from a situation and how these experiences provided opportunities for growth.

Matthew's consistent encouragement, even when I believed I was missing the mark, helped me to view myself and my work in a better light. The role of a school counselor, as we support students through a wide range of challenges, can be emotionally demanding. I always felt better after talking with Matthew. He had seen a lot during his many years as an educator, and his nonjudgmental stance allowed me to express myself in a way that brought my concerns into the open where I could make better sense of them.

Matthew also encouraged me to challenge him and to ask difficult questions when needed. If I didn't agree with or understand something Matthew said, he told me to bring it up and ask for clarification. Matthew's open and compassionate approach made me feel supported unconditionally, and the positive state of mind that emerged as a result strengthened my ability to tackle my daily challenges. To this day, whenever I am going through a rough time, I hear Matthew's kind, strong voice lifting my thoughts: *You're doing well, Daniel, and I'm proud of you.*

By consistently pointing me back to my strengths, allowing me to see the positive aspects of my experiences, and believing in me even when I struggled to believe in myself, Matthew let me know I could safely share anything and everything about my professional circumstances. Whatever I told him would always be met with kindness and helpful insight. As a result, my outlook was transformed. Through our mentoring relationship, I developed an ability to think more clearly and my growth was maximized.

Suggestions for Creating a Safe Place for Authentic Expression

The following list outlines specific suggestions for applying Caring Mentor Practice #2 in the areas of establishing trust, being available and dependable while maintaining confidentiality, validating your mentees' feelings, respecting your mentees as equal adults, offering encouragement, and seeing the best in your mentees.

Establish Trust with Your Mentees

- Set the tone at the beginning of your mentoring relationship with a conversation about trust.

- Back up your words through trustworthy actions.

- Remain nonjudgmental, humble, transparent, and consistent.

- Be an example of what it means to be a lifelong learner who is committed to ongoing personal growth and professional development.

Be Available and Dependable, and Maintain Confidentiality

- Make yourself available to your mentees by meeting consistently, either formally or informally.

- Maintain confidentiality but be sure your mentees are aware of the limits.

- Protect your time by ensuring you have a quiet place to meet where you are able to focus your full attention on the conversation.

- Keep your promises and respond to emails or phone calls within a reasonable amount of time.

Validate Your Mentees' Feelings

- When you notice your mentees are experiencing difficult emotions, invite them to share their feelings.

- Encourage your mentees to express themselves fully while you listen with a compassionate and nonjudgmental attitude.

- Identify the core emotion and, when appropriate, share similar emotional experiences to form a connection.

- Accept your mentees' feelings as they are without trying to fix or change them.

- After you have provided a safe place for your mentees to express their emotions, assist them in taking the next positive step forward.

Respect Your Mentees as Equal Adults

- Give your mentees the opportunity to make decisions about their own learning.

- Honor your mentees' knowledge and life experiences by getting to know them and their stories.

- Ensure that your mentoring work is relevant and applicable to real-life situations.

- Find out what motivates your mentees and incorporate those areas into your mentoring work.

- When possible, make your mentoring a collaborative process.

Be Encouraging and See the Best in Your Mentees

- Provide a variety of ways for your mentees to express themselves, whether this is in person, by telephone or video conference, or through writing.

- See the good in your mentees and help them to see the good in themselves by pointing out their positive qualities and how they are expressing those qualities through their work.

- Encourage your mentees to reflect on their daily experiences and guide them through the process of viewing their successes and challenges as learning experiences.

Bringing It All Together

Being a teacher or school counselor is challenging, to say the least, especially for new practitioners. Therefore, it's inevitable that mentees experience a wide range of emotions and sometimes feel overwhelmed. They need your emotional support. Providing a safe place for mentees to express themselves is key to establishing meaningful relationships that meet mentees where they are and help them take the next positive steps in their growth. When mentees feel emotionally safe, this encourages them to communicate in the ways necessary for mentors to understand their needs and support their success. In chapter 3, we discuss strategies mentors can employ to more effectively devote themselves to their mentees' ongoing growth.

CHAPTER 3

Caring Mentor Practice #3
*Caring Mentors Devote Themselves
to Their Mentees' Growth*

One of the foundational points I share when training new mentors is that the time we spend in the present moment, working directly with our mentees, is a vitally important component of the mentoring process. However, it is perhaps even more important that our work prepares mentees to succeed in the future when we will not always be there to support them. To ensure that mentees are learning and growing as a result of our mentoring relationships, caring mentors ask themselves two critical questions: *How will my mentees be different as a result of my mentoring?* and *What specific knowledge, skills, and attitudes will I help my mentees to develop that will contribute to their long-term success?* In this chapter, we examine powerful strategies to facilitate our mentees' growth, such as creating action plans, maintaining high expectations, and teaching by example.

Create Action Plans to Address Areas in Need of Improvement

Once, in the middle of the school year, I received a call from Mrs. West, a petite woman in her late thirties who was a new elementary school administrator. She asked for my assistance. From the serious tone of her voice, I knew we needed to meet as soon as possible. When we sat down in her office later that week, Mrs. West explained that Randy, her school counselor, was not performing well.

According to Mrs. West, Randy was receiving poor evaluations and was perceived as uncooperative by the administrative team. More important, he was not providing the school counseling services the children needed. Mrs. West had tried several times to talk with Randy in an attempt to understand what was happening, but these discussions did not lead to a change in his behavior or provide any evidence that he was working effectively with the students.

The next day, I visited Randy, a sturdy young man in his early twenties, and invited him for a walk across campus. As we strolled through the school's open-air hallways, I asked Randy to share his thoughts about how his work as a school counselor was progressing. With a sigh, he explained that he had been "seeing students," but the principal never recognized his efforts. Randy ran his fingers through his curly brown hair and shared that he felt misunderstood and isolated at school.

Randy also revealed that he didn't feel his college courses and subsequent internship at a high school had adequately prepared him for being a school counselor at the elementary level. It was clear that Randy needed assistance to develop a comprehensive, standards-based, data-driven school counseling program. He also needed strategies for communicating more effectively with his administration.

Knowing we first needed to confirm Randy was motivated and ready to learn, I asked him to tell me about the initial spark that led him to become a school counselor. As we took another lap around campus, Randy shared his belief that children need guidance to succeed academically, socially, and emotionally, and that all children deserve a good school counselor to be there for them.

When I asked Randy if he felt that he was maximizing his potential to provide these services, Randy explained that he felt badly because he knew he could do much more. It was important for me to clarify his perception of the challenges and barriers he faced before we worked on a solution. I suggested Randy rate his school counseling program on a scale of 0 to 10. A zero meant that he was not providing any services to students, and a 10 meant he was implementing the best school counseling program imaginable.

Randy gave himself a score of 4. I told him not to try to jump from a score of 4 to a score of 10 overnight, although we would

63

certainly strive for a 10 in the long run. Instead, the goal was to make small, sustainable changes by taking concrete actions to increase his effectiveness from a 4 to a 5. Once we reached a score of 5, we would work toward a score of 6 and continue to make small improvements with the aim of eventually reaching a 10.

Randy felt encouraged by this step-by-step approach and, standing a little taller, shared that he was ready to dive in. After reaffirming Randy's commitment to his professional growth and getting him in touch with his deeper professional purpose, we talked about building a more harmonious and productive relationship with Mrs. West.

I invited Randy to imagine asking Mrs. West about her vision and goals for the rest of the school year. I then explained that it would be critical that he listen carefully in order to understand what Mrs. West was trying to accomplish as an administrator. I suggested Randy let Mrs. West know his intention was to implement a school counseling program that would support her goals.

Initially, Randy was hesitant to have this conversation because he felt he might not be able to express himself effectively. I asked Randy if role-playing with me might help. Randy agreed, begrudgingly at first, but he committed to the exercise as a way of preparing for his meeting with Mrs. West.

Over the course of the next few days, we rehearsed the conversation several times in Randy's office. I took on the role of Mrs. West while Randy practiced speaking in a clear, friendly, and professional manner. After each practice, I offered Randy feedback. For example, I encouraged Randy to ask good follow-up questions to better understand Mrs. West's vision for the school. I also advised him to stick to his key talking points regarding his own ideas for the program and to provide specific examples of the activities he wanted to implement.

Randy felt more confident after our sessions and soon was ready to speak with Mrs. West in person. After their meeting, Randy reported that during his conversation with Mrs. West things immediately changed for the better. This interaction marked the first time Randy had reached out to Mrs. West to discuss how they could collaborate. Randy could tell Mrs. West appreciated his efforts to communicate. In fact, he had already requested a follow-up meeting to explore next steps.

To prepare for this meeting, Randy and I reviewed how to analyze the school's data and conduct a needs assessment in order to ensure his school counseling work would meet the specific needs of his students. I gave Randy some advice on how to use our district's computerized system to review students' academic, behavioral, and attendance data. I also helped Randy craft a needs assessment he could distribute to the staff and assisted him in creating a schedule for visiting with the different teams of teachers at his school. The purpose of these conversations was to discuss how the school counseling program could best help each grade level.

Randy followed through with this work, sending out the needs assessment survey and speaking with the teachers in every grade. He gathered valuable information and brought it to our next mentoring meeting. At that point, Randy and I sat down in his office, rolled up our sleeves, and developed a proposed calendar of activities for the remainder of the year.

I explained to Randy that one way of looking at school counseling is to view it as a series of six cups that we try to fill with as many quality activities as we can. The six cups represent individual counseling, group counseling, classroom lessons, school-wide initiatives, community initiatives, and the indirect services school counselors provide on behalf of students. These include facilitating parent-teacher conferences, connecting students and families with district or community resources, and consulting with teachers, administrators, and parents.

When the six cups are full that means a school counseling program is thriving. When the cups are empty or half-full that means students are missing key services needed to support their success and well-being. Although most school counselors find it difficult to keep each of the six cups full at all times, analyzing the degree to which they have been filled provides a helpful gauge for recognizing success and identifying areas in need of improvement.

Randy loved this approach, and we collaborated on daily, weekly, and monthly schedules incorporating each of these six components. It was important that I showed Randy how much I believed in him by encouraging him to play an active role in establishing his vision. I made sure he took the lead in the planning process whenever possible while offering feedback to support his success. When Randy was ready, he met with Mrs. West and shared his proposed plan. Mrs. West was happy with the plan, which Randy began to implement at his school.

I also suggested Randy use a form I had created to make notes about each of his activities within the six cups so he could share this information with Mrs. West at their weekly team meetings. Randy used the form consistently to share successes, outline challenges, and collaborate with his team on solutions. After a few weeks, I received an email from Mrs. West telling me that Randy was doing an outstanding job at his school. He provided excellent school counseling services to his students, he communicated effectively, and she and Randy were now working together beautifully.

Randy also sent me an email, and he attached a document he had made representing the six cups visually. He told me to feel free to share this document with other counselors. I did, and many other counselors have found Randy's document useful as well. Randy is now a successful school counselor, has an effective working relationship with his administration, and is an active member of our district's school counseling leadership team where he assists other counselors in organizing programs and communicating with their administrations.

In Randy's case, it was clear that caring mentoring needed to take the form of coaching and direct instruction to enhance his professional growth. The first step was to help Randy remember why he had become a school counselor. By asking Randy to tell me what had inspired him to enter the profession, I gave him the opportunity to reflect on the deeper meaning of his work. Clarifying his professional purpose provided Randy with the energy and enthusiasm he needed to learn and grow—a point I address in greater detail in chapter 4. Randy also needed the knowledge and skills to effectively collaborate with his administration. Bolstering Randy's communication skills required explicit teaching, so I provided tools and resources, helped him practice through role play, and offered both corrective feedback and ongoing encouragement.

Maintain High Expectations

Another mentor I had early in my school counseling career was Ms. Quinn, a principal who was a rising star at the school level and is now a district leader. As a school administrator, Ms. Quinn expected superior performance in every aspect of my work. I remember when she first introduced herself to our staff in the school's media center. Standing tall, she said clearly and without apology, "Hold me accountable for excellence, because I can promise I will hold you accountable for excellence."

And that is exactly what Ms. Quinn did. As part of my role as a school counselor, I was tasked with coordinating the school's awards assemblies. Ms. Quinn expected everything to be perfect, from the invitations to the music to the staging to the speeches. She observed each aspect of my work closely, and we met in her office after each assembly to debrief. Although Ms. Quinn pointed out the things I did well, she always shared specific ideas about how I could improve.

Once Ms. Quinn told me, "Danny, our awards ceremonies are just as important as a wedding or any other significant life event for our children and families." Ms. Quinn emphasized how our work impacted others—a lesson that has become a foundational part of my approach to mentoring.

Ms. Quinn's mentoring also took the form of weekly meetings to check on my progress. We reviewed the list of my school counseling responsibilities and discussed each one, looking for ways to elevate my work to the next level. At first, I felt defensive and wondered, *Will Ms. Quinn ever think my work is good enough?* However, as I got to know Ms. Quinn better, I understood and appreciated that she wanted me to do my best, not only for myself but for the benefit of our students.

Ms. Quinn taught me that an essential aspect of caring mentoring is a desire for your mentees to grow and succeed. This desire, however, is not always expressed through sentimentality. Sometimes the deepest care takes the form of tough love. This point was reinforced when I researched my dissertation. Tabitha, a new teacher mentee I interviewed, asserted, "I don't think that caring is always what most people perceive to be caring. Because you're nice to someone or really sweet to someone, that is not necessarily caring to me. I think that caring, if you actually care about someone, you are making your best efforts to make them the best that they can be."

All too often teachers and school counselors confuse care with "niceness." Sometimes care means giving constructive criticism, showing your mentees what is working or not working and why. In many cases, bringing out the best in mentees requires challenging conversations, which may be uncomfortable. It is essential, however, that these interactions include specific suggestions for how to improve.

Ms. Quinn set high expectations for me and took the time to make sure I was meeting them. I can hear her still as she told me, *You need to inspect what it is you expect.* Looking back, I realize Ms. Quinn demanded excellence because she saw untapped potential in me that she wanted to bring to life. I would never have become an educational leader had it not been for Ms. Quinn's dedication to my professional development.

Deciding whether to apply a tough love approach or a more nurturing style of mentoring requires the mentor to take into account the personality of the mentee and the ways in which he or she is motivated. Some mentees need a gentle push to improve, while others require a more direct challenge in order to rise to the next level. What's important is the mentor's intention, which should be focused on the well-being and professional growth of the mentee. Mentors should give careful consideration to which style of mentoring best expresses care in a given situation.

Mentors should also observe the effects of their mentoring actions in order to learn which methods garner the best results. Asking mentees questions such as "Would it be okay if I challenge you a bit here?" or "How did it feel when I challenged you during our session today?" provides key information to help mentors adjust their approach.

Capitalize on Teachable Moments and Be a Positive Role Model

The ability to recognize and make the most of teachable moments is another powerful quality of caring mentors. Teachable moments are usually unplanned occurrences in which mentors have the opportunity to share knowledge or teach skills in response to an event. This information is not usually found in textbooks. Instead, it is hard-won wisdom that comes directly from the mentor's experience. Teachable moments are also a chance for mentors to demonstrate key ideas as they lead by example.

As we sat on the bleachers overlooking the football field, I spoke with Grant, a high school reading teacher who was receiving support from his mentor, Mr. Livingston. "Whenever I would have difficulty with certain students in the classroom," Grant said, "he always told me to give him a call first. He didn't want me to call the office, because he wanted to show me how to handle the situation." Grant shared that Mr. Livingston used every opportunity to teach, especially those that involved students getting into what many educators would call "trouble."

Mr. Livingston taught Grant that when students act out in class it is often a call for help. Grant explained, "He showed me that sometimes students are acting out because of something they're struggling with inside. If we write a discipline referral right away, we might miss the opportunity to get to the root of issue." Mr. Livingston taught Grant that although it may appear on the surface as if a student is being disrespectful, he or she is really reaching out to say, *Please help me.*

After a brief pause, Grant reflected on how he had become a better educator by learning from Mr. Livingston. The kindness Mr. Livingston extended toward his students inspired Grant to extend that same kindness to his own students. Grant said, "What I learned most from Mr. Livingston is that students can't learn when their personal or emotional needs aren't met. He also added, "A lot of the time students are hungry, tired, stressed, or are not feeling safe." Grant explained that he stays calm when students misbehave, asks questions, builds relationships, and recognizes that every moment in the classroom is a chance to change a life.

Teach the Fundamentals and Support Your Mentees in Gaining Independence

I spoke with Vanessa, a middle school language arts teacher in her early thirties who had aspirations of becoming an administrator, one October via video conference. As we settled down in front of our computer screens, I asked her to tell me about the mentoring she had received as a new educator. Vanessa explained how her mentor, Ms. Hill, focused on imparting the fundamentals of effective teaching and helped Vanessa gain independence as a classroom instructor.

Ms. Hill told Vanessa at the beginning of their relationship that although she'd be available for support when Vanessa needed her that her mentoring was a temporary arrangement designed to help Vanessa grow into an independent, successful teacher. Ms. Hill provided Vanessa with direct instruction on effective classroom practices and then allowed her the space to teach so that she could master these new skills.

I was curious as to how Ms. Hill went about teaching these skills, and so I asked Vanessa to tell me more about her interactions with Ms. Hill. After taking a moment to consider this, Vanessa described how Ms. Hill watched her instruction closely, then made time to discuss the specific elements that went well and what could be improved.

For example, Vanessa related how she had the tendency to stand in one place while teaching and that she needed to move around the classroom more to keep students engaged. To address this issue, Ms. Hill charted Vanessa's movements over the course of a lesson. After the lesson, she showed Vanessa which parts of the room she occupied while teaching and which areas she neglected to visit. Then, after school, Ms. Hill had Vanessa teach a practice lesson. Ms. Hill gave Vanessa feedback to ensure she was positioning herself effectively as she taught. As a result of Ms. Hill's instruction, Vanessa has now mastered this skill and applies it naturally when she's teaching.

Another example of how Ms. Hill fostered Vanessa's growing independence was the way Ms. Hill helped Vanessa become proficient at organizing field trips. "The first time I had to organize a field trip," Vanessa said, "Ms. Hill completed the entire procedure with me. The second time, she guided me through it but made sure I did the work myself. She'd say, 'Here's the paperwork, now what do you do,' inviting me to try it until I became competent." By guiding Vanessa through the steps, then relinquishing control, Ms. Hill helped Vanessa reach the point where she could complete the process without needing assistance.

Vanessa pointed out that when mentors provide too much unrequested assistance, their efforts can become harmful rather than helpful. From her perspective, professional growth is a process of trial and error that requires mentors to allow mentees to learn from their own experiences. In Vanessa's view, caring mentoring should not be about "trying to do the job for you" but rather "giving you the opportunity to make mistakes and learn."

To further illustrate this point, Vanessa told me about a class she had that was unmotivated and underachieving. The assistant principal showed up and, instead of giving Vanessa ideas to improve the situation in a private conversation, the assistant principal tried to motivate the class on her own.

Vanessa massaged her temples as she said, "I needed ideas about how to keep that class motivated, not for her to come in and take control. I just needed some guidance, but after she took over that day, it took me a long time to gain the leadership back with that class." Ms. Hill's approach, however, was very different than that of the assistant principal's. As Vanessa put it, "A caring mentor is someone who's there when you need them but not overwhelming or hovering over you."

Ms. Hill taught Vanessa the fundamentals of effective classroom instruction. These strategies helped Vanessa succeed with her students. However, once Vanessa understood the concepts, Ms. Hill knew Vanessa needed to apply them in her classroom and experiment with the students' responses while learning to make adjustments on her own. It also helped that Ms. Hill told Vanesa from the start that her mentorship would end once it was no longer needed. This allowed them to put their relationship in context and prepared them both for the ways their relationship would change as Vanessa grew as an independent teacher.

Formal mentoring usually begins and ends at prescribed times, often starting at the beginning of the school year and finishing at the end. Informal mentoring, on the other hand, is initiated whenever the need arises and comes to a close once the need no longer exists. In either case, it's important to address early on in the process how the mentorship will come to a close. This topic needs to be discussed all throughout the relationship, and these conversations set the stage for a positive closure. I discuss this subject in more depth in the final section of this book.

One of the primary purposes of any mentoring relationship is to support mentees as they take the next steps in achieving autonomy. This requires mentors to provide direct instruction followed by opportunities for their mentees to succeed or temporarily fail on their own. Allowing mentees to, at times, struggle independently gives them a chance to think critically and develop problem-solving skills that lead to further growth. As a follow-up to these experiences, it's important to teach your mentees to reflect on what they are learning from their challenges and successes. To accomplish this, I often use the following questions as prompts:

- What do you think went well during that activity?

- Why do you think that approach worked well?

- What skills did you employ that you can use in other situations?

- What didn't go well during that activity?

- Why didn't it go well?

- What can you learn from this experience and do differently next time?

Facilitating a process of instruction, analysis, and reflection promotes self-sufficiency in mentees. Although it takes time, the goal is for mentees to develop into competent, responsible professionals who have secured the foundational skills needed to move toward independence and mastery. By gradually providing Vanessa with opportunities to work through challenges in the classroom and in her other school responsibilities, Ms. Hill allowed her to develop the strength and confidence that only comes through the direct experience of working through tasks on one's own.

Suggestions for Devoting Yourself to Your Mentees' Growth

The following list outlines specific suggestions for applying Caring Mentor Practice #3 in the realms of identifying areas in need of improvement, creating actions plans, maintaining high expectations, capitalizing on teachable moments, being a role model, teaching the fundamentals, and supporting your mentees as they gain independence.

Identify Areas in Need of Improvement and Create an Action Plan

- Invite your mentees to explore and rekindle the initial spark that inspired them to become teachers or school counselors by asking questions about what motivated them to enter the profession.

- Have your mentees assess their current level of progress and take specific actions to improve, remembering that smaller steps designed to be sustained over time are the most effective.

- Teach your mentees skills such as setting objectives, organizing lessons, managing time, asking open-ended questions, paraphrasing, and assessing needs while also providing opportunities for practice and feedback.

78

- Encourage your mentees by celebrating their improvements and successes.

Maintain High Expectations

- Hold your mentees accountable by having them set daily or weekly goals and tracking their progress. I list two useful apps for tracking goals in the Suggested Reading and Resources section at the end of this book.

- Observe your mentees' work and set up regular meeting times to provide constructive feedback.

- Remember that expressing care sometimes requires challenging conversations in order to foster your mentees' growth.

- Let the personalities of your mentees determine how to best challenge them to grow by asking questions, observing the effects of your mentoring practices, gathering feedback, and adjusting your approach to meet your mentees' unique needs.

Capitalize on Teachable Moments and Be a Positive Role Model

- Identify teachable moments and capitalize on these opportunities by providing instruction and encouraging your mentees to reflect on what they are learning.

- Collaborate with your mentees on projects or activities to provide firsthand experience applying new skills and concepts.

- Remember that the most powerful example you can set as a mentor is through your actions, whether it is by serving as a strong role model or by putting your own suggestions into practice.

Teach the Fundamentals and Support Your Mentees in Gaining Independence

- Provide direct instruction to help your mentees master the fundamentals.

- Ask your mentees thoughtful questions to encourage reflection and self-analysis.

- Take time to discuss when and how the mentoring relationship will come to an end to ensure that closure will be a positive experience.

- Support your mentees as they move toward increased professional autonomy.

Bringing It All Together

In this chapter, we explored the idea that the work of caring mentors is not limited to making our mentees feel better through a supportive relationship. Caring mentoring builds on our bonds with our mentees by focusing on specific ways to help them learn and grow. This in turn allows our mentees to benefit from the instruction we provide, develop the ability to assess themselves, learn to maximize their progress, challenge themselves to meet our high expectations, and gain a sense of self-sufficiency that will last throughout their careers. In chapter 4, we examine another key component of care that is often neglected in mentoring relationships: sharing meaningful perspectives and insights with mentees.

CHAPTER 4

Caring Mentor Practice #4

*Caring Mentors Share Their Perspectives
and Insights with Their Mentees*

As we've discussed, teachers and school counselors face a host of challenges as they navigate their first years in the educational profession. As mentors help new educators overcome these difficulties and learn to thrive, they have a unique opportunity to share the lessons they have learned.

By sharing their perspectives and insights, mentors help their mentees view themselves and the situations they encounter in truer, healthier, and more beneficial ways. In this chapter, we unpack ways to assist mentees as they discover the deeper purpose of their work, identify core professional values, cope with difficulties, and take advantage of opportunities to succeed.

Help Your Mentees Remember Their Why

Michelle, a talented elementary school counselor with more than twenty years of experience, pulled me aside after a training session to ask me to mentor her through a difficult time. She was feeling overwhelmed and exhausted by her workload due to an increase in student issues at her school. Although Michelle enjoyed her work, she felt discouraged and was considering an early retirement.

When I visited Michelle at her school to discuss her situation, we sat down in a quiet corner of the media center to talk. She folded her hands on top of the wooden table and, for several minutes, shared her struggles and frustrations with the career for which she once held a passion. In addition to the stress she experienced during a typical day, Michelle was also concerned about the kind of school counselor she was becoming. She felt less compassion for the students than she once had, and she had reservations about remaining at a job that brought out these feelings.

It was clear that even though Michelle was having difficulties, she still loved her students and had a lot to offer as a school counselor. While practical adjustments to her approach might have helped a little, the core of Michelle's issue required us to explore her perspectives about herself, her role as a school counselor, and the deeper purpose of her life and work.

I was reminded of Simon Sinek's TED Talk "How Great Leaders Inspire Action." Simon Sinek worked as a motivational business consultant, and his philosophy for motivating others revolved around the idea that many people emphasize what they are doing and how they are doing it but never focus on why they are doing it.

I shared the following story with Michelle. During a Saturday morning walk, just as the sun floated over the lake near my home, I stopped to watch a confrontation between two birds. One was a little bird, no bigger than my hand, and the other was a great hawk with piercing eyes, a bulging chest, and a wide wingspan. When the hawk swooped in a graceful arc to perch at the top of a pine tree, the little bird skittered in pursuit, flapping around it, and eventually chasing it from the tree. The hawk then flew to another tree, and again the little bird drove the hawk away. What struck me was how the little bird, a pocket-sized creature, seemed to dominate the hawk, a powerful and majestic predator.

I considered the little bird, which must have been one-fifth the size of the hawk. The hawk could have devoured the little bird, and yet the little bird held sway over the hawk for at least two minutes. Finally, the hawk glided across the lake, becoming smaller and smaller until it vanished from sight.

As I pondered how such a bizarre turn of events could occur, I heard high-pitched chirps from a nearby oak tree. In the branches, I saw a nest filled with baby chicks. I realized that the little bird was their mother and that nothing and no one, no matter how big or strong or fierce, was going to hurt her babies. The little bird carried a clear sense of purpose— to protect the life of her children—and in that moment, she became unstoppable.

When I finished this story, Michelle sat quietly, clearly touched but still struggling with her dilemma. I asked her to take out a piece of paper and guided her through through an exercise I call Remember Your Why. I invited Michelle to close her eyes and think about what she really wanted in her life and work. I told her to write from the heart about her purpose as a school counselor and why the work was important to her. Michelle, a bit hesitant, took a deep breath and began to write. She wrote for several minutes without stopping. When she was finished, she looked up with tears in her eyes.

I asked Michelle how she was feeling. "Relieved," she said. She had been running from one emergency to the next and hadn't had a chance to reflect on the deeper meaning of her work. As she started writing about her purpose, she remembered how, as a little girl, she had no one to turn to at school. Things had been tough at home when Michelle was a child, and she remembered the adults in her life always being busy with things that seemed to be more important than she was.

Michelle had longed for a caring adult to talk to but couldn't remember feeling safe enough to open up to anyone. By the time she started college, she knew she wanted to become a school counselor so that she could be the caring adult children depended on at school.

I asked Michelle to summarize this insight in a single sentence she could remember and carry with her. "My purpose," she said, "is to be the caring adult for my students that I never had." Seeing the powerful impact this realization had upon Michelle, I urged her to read and reflect on that statement every morning before she worked with her students. When I followed up with her a few days later, she shared how she had begun to see her students' discipline issues as opportunities to connect rather than problems. By shifting her perspective, Michelle renewed her energy and recommitted herself to her passion for school counseling.

My first step in working with Michelle was to listen carefully to her perspective. A thorough understanding of her point of view better equipped me to help her clarify her thinking and share my own perspectives in order to shed light on her situation. It was also important for me to recognize Michelle's good intentions, despite her frustrations. By telling Michelle a story to which she could relate, I helped her reflect on the deeper meaning of her work. I then guided her through the Remember Your Why exercise and assisted her in connecting with the spark that had led her to her career. This motivated her to work through what had seemed like an insurmountable challenge.

I made a point to recognize and acknowledge Michelle's positive intentions when she expressed the difficult emotions with which she was struggling. Often, especially when under stress, our minds gravitate toward the challenges we're facing instead of seeing the whole picture. In Michelle's case, she was so focused on the problems she was facing that she couldn't recognize the goodness within herself, let alone within her students.

As I guided Michelle through the process of clarifying her perspective, while sharing my own, she reconnected with the reason she had become a school counselor. It was important that, as Michelle's mentor, I served as a mirror, reflecting the positive intentions that were always within her but had been hidden by her overwhelming workload.

Guide Your Mentees in Identifying and Expressing Their Values

Helping mentees clarify their values is essential to the mentoring process. When mentees understand their values, they can use them as a compass to inform their choices and direct their actions, especially during times of stress or uncertainty. Often mentees' emotions, as well as those of students, families, and colleagues, run high during the course of a school year. Remembering their values in these moments provides mentees with an anchor to help them stay centered in who they are and what they truly believe in.

After her first month as a school counselor, one of my mentees called to tell me she felt overwhelmed by what she considered her school's "negative environment." Allison, a young lady who always greeted me with a smile, said her school had hired a brand-new administrative team and that a group of veteran teachers refused to cooperate with the administration's new policies, creating tension.

Allison, who was trying to establish herself in her own career, felt trapped in the middle of a power struggle. As a school counselor, she wasn't a teacher, but she wasn't an administrator either. When teachers or administrators came to her office to vent, she felt conflicted about how to respond, as this left her "stuck in the middle." Allison saw the merit of the teachers' arguments, but she also wanted to remain loyal to her administrative team. Exasperated, she told me, "I'm getting distracted from my work, and I don't know where I stand."

Allison's predicament reminded me of an incident from my own career. When we sat down in her office that afternoon, I shared the following story.

When I first started my teaching career as an adjunct professor, I used to visit a little store on the university campus and pick up a quick snack before class. The same woman worked at the checkout every day. She always furrowed her brow and scowled as she snatched the items from her customers' hands and threw them down on the counter with a loud bang.

When it was my turn, I tried to smile and say hello, but this woman always responded with a menacing glare. I began to anticipate these uncomfortable exchanges and raised my internal defenses each time I approached the counter. *I'll just make my purchase and get out*, I thought. A wall developed around my heart, which limited my sense of freedom and well-being.

One day, as I waited in line at the store, I thought more deeply about this woman. I wondered what she had gone through or might be currently experiencing that caused her to feel so angry. I thought about times in my own life when I struggled and how difficult that was. I imagined what this woman's feet must feel like, standing behind the counter all day long, serving one customer after another.

Do I have to close down when I interact with this woman? I wondered. *Do I have to let another person's state of mind take me away from who I really am and who I want to be? Was it really necessary to defend myself in this situation?* I considered how, instead of protecting myself, I might stay true to myself in relation to this woman. When I arrived at my desk that day, I wrote out a list of values that represented who I believed I truly was and who I aspired to be. The first three words that came to mind were kindness, respect, and openness.

The next day, I walked into the store determined to express those three qualities, regardless of how the woman responded. I smiled at her and said hello. Most important, I kept my heart open throughout our entire interaction. I'd love to say that the woman and I shared a warm hug and developed a lifelong friendship. The truth is she continued to act as she always had. The difference was that, from then on, I did my best to let my deepest values guide me rather than allow her actions and reactions to control me.

Allison's face brightened as I shared this story. We both knew we needed to identify her deepest values and she needed to focus on expressing them during challenging moments at work. I asked Allison to take a few deep breaths, close her eyes, and reflect on who she aspired to be, both as a person and as a school counselor.

I then invited Allison to write down her top three personal values. After a few minutes, she shared what she had written: honest, accepting, and supportive. I suggested Allison use the acronym HAS to remember these values, and I encouraged her to write more about what each one meant to her. How, I asked her, could she express these values in her work with students and staff?

After Allison completed this exercise, she explained that the word *honest* meant being truthful with herself and others about her thoughts and feelings. *Accepting* meant embracing her feelings and the feelings of others without judging them. Lastly, *supportive* meant being present and kind, not only to herself but to others as they navigated the challenges at her school.

Allison later told me that this exercise transformed her outlook at work. Although the situation between the teachers and administration was still tense, Allison anchored herself in her own values rather than being pushed off-center by the strong viewpoints and emotions of others.

I frequently recommend this important exercise when I work with other teacher and school counselor mentors. I ask mentors, either in an individual or group session, to take a few quiet moments to turn inward. I ask the mentors to reflect on the good qualities they possess and what kind of person and mentor they want to become. After guiding them through a series of deep breaths to establish a sense of centered presence, I invite them to write down the top three values they strive to express as a mentor.

I then ask them to write about why they chose each of these values. Afterward, if they feel comfortable doing so, I invite them to share their thoughts. The mentors often discover in this exercise a renewed sense of clarity about who they are. Some of the common values that emerge are compassion, kindness, love, honesty, integrity, creativity, patience, understanding, and the desire for ongoing growth. When mentors clarify their values, they report they are better able to react to stressful situations by expressing the values they've identified as most helpful and true.

Provide Reassurance and Impart Wisdom from Your Own Experiences

Reassuring mentees provides them with much-needed support as they navigate the inevitable frustrations of their new professional roles. Pointing out their positive qualities and acknowledging their success mitigates feelings of discouragement. When mentees know we as mentors have experienced similar challenges, this provides them with a sense of hope and confidence.

Lia, a calm and gentle young woman, was hired as an elementary school counselor after serving as a high school teacher for three years. She had no experience working at the elementary level and, being new to the position, was nervous about "failing as a school counselor."

I began to mentor Lia, who struggled with a lack of self-confidence. She believed she was making progress with her students, both individually and in small groups. However, when she asked other staff members to participate in school-wide initiatives, such as her kindness campaign or career day efforts, they showed no interest in contributing.

We walked across her school campus one sunny afternoon and found a shaded picnic table near the recess area. When we sat down to talk, Lia told me she felt rejected by her colleagues and was starting to doubt her ability to succeed as a school counselor. As a result, she felt increasingly isolated and didn't believe the other staff members considered her efforts worthwhile.

Having experienced similar challenges with staff participation at the beginning of my career, I knew Lia's dilemma required a shift in perspective. I shared that I too had felt a sense of rejection when teachers didn't, at first, participate in my school-wide initiatives. I realized, however, their lack of involvement derived from their packed schedules and the timing of my requests rather than any judgments about me or the quality of my work.

As a first step, I reassured Lia that she would become a successful school counselor and that she had much to offer in her new role. I saw how much she truly loved the students, and I told her how much I appreciated the chance to work with such a caring person. Her passion for learning and her determination to make a difference in her school inspired me, even in the short time I had known her. As I shared some of the wonderful attributes I saw in Lia, her spirits lifted.

I also needed to help Lia take ownership of her success, so I asked her to tell me about the progress she was making with her students. She closed her eyes for a moment to collect her thoughts. She then explained she had already developed strong connections with the children and that they enjoyed working with her. Lia told me about several effective academic and behavioral plans she had implemented. Her group work provided a safe place for students to open up about painful situations at home. As I helped Lia shift her focus away from her feelings of rejection and toward her talents and the positive impact she was having in her new position, she took on a new energy.

Emphasizing Lia's positive qualities showed her she was on the right track and helped her acknowledge her own success. At this point, we were ready to explore the challenge of getting more staff to participate in her school-wide initiatives. I asked Lia to tell me more about how she had reached out to teachers. Lia had tried to recruit teachers to help with her initiatives during their staff meetings after school, but she hadn't received any support.

I had taken a similar approach as a new school counselor and found that it was more effective to ask teachers for help individually or in smaller groups. Also, when I approached teachers on employee planning days, the days they usually felt less stressed and overwhelmed, they were more likely to say yes. I suggested that Lia ask teachers what kinds of projects she could do to be of help to them.

Lia tried these strategies and soon saw positive results. Teachers were open to talking about her projects when they had more time, and the individual conversations allowed them to ask her more detailed questions and get to know Lia better. Soon, Lia had gathered a full team of teachers for her kindness committee. Teachers also pitched in to support her efforts to recruit community members for career day.

By changing her perspective, Lia improved her view of herself as a capable school counselor, formed a stronger connection with her colleagues, and received increased support for her school-wide initiatives. This shift would not have taken place if I hadn't showed Lia that I believed in her and acknowledged the great work she was already doing with her students. Lia's struggle with self-confidence and the lack of support she had received from her colleagues diverted her attention from the progress she was making, causing her to doubt herself and her work.

When Lia considered the progress she was making with her students and heard how I had struggled with the same issues as a new counselor, she felt reassured and began to appreciate the positive strides she had made. In addition, my experiences helped Lia realize that her colleagues' apparent lack of interest in collaborating with her was not personal. Armed with this new perspective, Lia felt empowered to reach out to her colleagues again, and this time she was met with the support she needed.

One of the key roles of a caring mentor is to reassure mentees that it's okay and even natural to feel overwhelmed, anxious, and afraid. The first year of teaching or school counseling is often filled with stress and uncertainty. Reassurance from a trusted mentor helps mentees to view setbacks as learning experiences rather than indications that they are failing.

My mentees often share their sense of relief once they understand they don't have to be perfect. My research and experiences have taught me it usually takes new educators a few years to feel competent. Becoming an effective teacher or school counselor is a challenging process that requires time and patience.

I've witnessed firsthand the power of telling our mentees that we believe in them and that we will be there to support them when they struggle. New teachers and counselors often grapple with self-doubt, but when they know their mentors believe in them and will be present for the long haul, they feel motivated to move forward and grow as a professional.

Share Information About Yourself for Your Mentees' Benefit

I met with Grant, the high school reading teacher we discussed in chapter 3, on a warm afternoon in early August. We sat on the aluminum bleachers, looking out over the school's football field, under the shade of the press box. I asked Grant to tell me more about his experiences as a mentee. Grant shared that his mentor, Mr. Livingston, used the life experiences they had in common to form a bond with him at the outset of their relationship. Smiling widely, he said, "We both were former athletes and both coached track and field. We were also both African American men and fathers. Mr. Livingston always used to ask me questions about my time as a runner and about how my coaching was going and about my family."

When I asked Grant to tell me about the impact of Mr. Livingston's approach, Grant explained that by focusing on their common interests in sports and fatherhood, Mr. Livingston helped Grant feel more comfortable sharing personal information. "The fact," he said, "that I was a male and he was a male, that I was a minority and he was a minority, that I was a father and he was a father, all of that helped us to relate to each other."

To learn how Mr. Livingston built on his initial connection with Grant, I asked Grant to share a typical mentoring conversation. Grant leaned forward and said that Mr. Livingston frequently used real-life stories as teaching points. Mr. Livingston had told him that, growing up in poverty, he had to wear the same pair of shoes several years in a row, even when they became too small. Grant said he felt a strong emotional connection with Mr. Livingston when he related how other students made fun of him as a child and how that strengthened his resolve to succeed in life.

Mr. Livingston's willingness to tell Grant about the difficult moments in his life and the lessons he'd learned from them inspired Grant to share more of his own story with his students. "Because of the way Mr. Livingston talked with me about his life," Grant said, "I told him more about mine, and one day in class I decided to tell my students about me being adopted."

When Grant learned about the power of self-disclosure from Mr. Livingston, Grant developed the courage to open up about his own life experiences, first within their mentoring relationship and then by sharing his story with his class. After a long pause, Grant added, "Later on I found out that one of my students actually got accepted to college after writing an admissions essay about my teaching. She had written about how open and honest I was and how she was adopted too and had been so afraid to tell people until she heard me talk about it." Mr. Livingston's willingness to share information about himself for the benefit of his mentee led to a transformational moment that brought Grant's teaching to the next level.

As we can see from Mr. Livingston's work with Grant, mentoring from the inside out is more than just exchanging information. This approach requires a bond between the mentor and mentee that allows their inner worlds to be open to one another. If Mr. Livingston had rushed directly into pedagogically focused mentoring, Grant would not initially have been ready to receive his instruction. Instead, Mr. Livingston showed his sincere interest by asking questions and uncovering what life circumstances they had in common.

Another way Mr. Livingston became better acquainted with Grant was through sharing his life stories. When Mr.

Livingston disclosed some of the difficulties he encountered growing up, Grant became more comfortable discussing his own vulnerabilities. In fact, Mr. Livingston's candidness empowered Grant to incorporate more of his own life experiences into his teaching.

Mr. Livingston's self-disclosure had a clear purpose. He didn't view these conversations as opportunities to vent or to pass the time. Instead, he related his life experiences with the goal of helping Grant share his own story and thus grow into his potential.

Introduce Your Mentees to New and Empowering Possibilities

One evening, after a community event at his school, I interviewed Zachary, a veteran high school math teacher. Zachary had struggled during his first few years of teaching, and I wanted to better understand how he worked through his challenges and became successful in his career. We pulled out a couple of chairs in his classroom, and he shared that early on as a teacher he felt frustrated because he wasn't getting through to his students or growing professionally. Zachary stroked his neatly trimmed beard and told me that when he expressed these feelings to his mentor, Mrs. Clay, she shared something that changed his life and career.

I asked what specifically she had done to help him. Zachary smiled and reported that Mrs. Clay had felt the same at one point in her journey. She shared how she went back to school after several years of teaching to earn her master's degree. Zachary leaned in and explained Mrs. Clay had not been certain she could succeed in her own education while working full-time. Even still, she had pushed through and she encouraged him to do the same.

What else, I asked, had Mrs. Clay said that gave Zachary the needed boost to take action? Zachary said, "Mrs. Clay pushed me to become an expert in my field because it would not only elevate my career and help me to grow professionally, but it would give me more to offer my students." Mrs. Clay also pointed out Zachary's strong work ethic and his ability to learn new material quickly. These words of affirmation gave Zachary the extra confidence he needed to continue his education.

By sharing her experiences, Mrs. Clay illuminated an educational pathway Zachary had not previously considered. She outlined the struggles she overcame and the ways in which she profited from going back to school. Mrs. Clay also described the benefits Zachary would receive by pursuing a higher degree and reassured him that he had what it took to succeed.

Because Mrs. Clay encouraged Zachary to pursue his master's degree, in part by sharing her own story, he gained the confidence he needed to take his career to the next level. For

Zachary, his mentoring conversations with Mrs. Clay were the turning point in his career.

Like an experienced mountain guide who has already traversed the rocky slopes, caring mentors take care to point out the pitfalls that will be part of their mentees' journeys. Mentors help their mentees avoid dangerous areas while illuminating opportunities to climb higher. As a result of Mrs. Clay's guidance, Zachary now holds his master's degree and is an effective, fulfilled teacher who enjoys his work.

Suggestions for Sharing Perspectives and Insights with Mentees

The following list outlines specific suggestions for applying Caring Mentor Practice #4 in the areas of helping mentees to remember their why, providing reassurance, imparting wisdom from your own experiences, sharing information about yourself for your mentees' benefit, and introducing mentees to new and empowering possibilities.

Guide Your Mentees through the Remember Your Why Exercise
- Identify your mentees' positive intentions by asking them to share why they first decided to become a teacher or school counselor and what about their job means the most to them.

- Invite your mentees to write about their why.

- Provide opportunities for your mentees to reflect on their why and challenge them to revisit their why on a consistent basis.

- Share insights into your own why with your mentees.

Guide Your Mentees through the Values Exercise

- Have your mentees write a list of their deepest values, the meanings behind those values, and why those values are important to them.

- Ask your mentees to reflect on each of their chosen values and visualize how they can apply them to challenging situations at work.

- Share your own values, along with stories, perspectives, and insights, to motivate your mentees and encourage thoughtful conversation.

Provide Reassurance and Impart Wisdom from Your Own Experiences

- Reassure your mentees by expressing your appreciation for them and helping them recognize their success and progress.

- Let your mentees know you believe in them. Help them understand that making mistakes and learning from those mistakes is an essential part of growth.

- Let your mentees know that it is natural to feel a range of emotions during their first challenging years in the profession and that things will improve over time.

- Share challenges you encountered and the solutions you applied to overcome them.

Share Information About Yourself for Your Mentees' Benefit

- Discuss common interests and life circumstances to form a strong bond with your mentees.

- Tell stories about challenges you have faced to let your mentees know they're not alone in their struggles.

- Talk about some of your successes to inspire your mentees and pass along the lessons you have learned.

- Avoid venting or relating stories that are not relevant to your mentees' growth.

- Remember that the purpose of disclosing information about yourself is to support your mentees' development and success.

Introduce Your Mentees to New and Empowering Possibilities

- Share your experiences, perspectives, and insights to help your mentees view their situations in more helpful and more empowering ways.

- Challenge your mentees to take action and reach their potential by setting meaningful goals.

- Share the lessons you have learned during your professional journey and explore how those lessons might apply to your mentees' journeys.

Bringing It All Together

One of the most powerful opportunities we have as mentors is to express care to our mentees by sharing helpful perspectives and insights. As experienced educators, we've collected a wealth of experience. We can use the knowledge we've gained on our professional paths to help mentees view themselves and their work in healthier, truer, and more beneficial ways. Additionally, we have the chance to support our mentees by helping them develop their own perspectives. In chapter 5, we investigate what it means to take effective action on behalf of our mentees.

CHAPTER 5

Caring Mentor Practice #5

Caring Mentors Act on Behalf of Their Mentees

The ways in which we listen, speak, and relate to our mentees allow us to make connections that open the door for effective teaching, learning, and professional development. Since new educators, however, are often in difficult and vulnerable positions, effective care also requires us to take concrete action to support their needs.

In this chapter, we look at actions that mentors can take to help their mentees succeed, including advocacy, providing opportunities for leadership experiences, sharing resources, and assisting mentees in finding a sense of belonging.

Advocate for Your Mentees

At twenty-two, Faith was fresh out of college. As a new elementary school counselor, she was ready to implement a research-based school counseling program. But when she started work at her school, the principal allotted most of her time to duties that did not fall under the job description of a school counselor. For example, Faith was asked to supervise morning and afternoon traffic, monitor the cafeteria, coordinate tests, perform clerical work, and act as a substitute teacher. To add to her challenges, the previous counselor who had served in Faith's position had performed the job for decades in exactly this way.

Over the course of our mentoring relationship, I met with Faith in her office. Piles of papers covered her desk. Stacks of cardboard boxes filled with standardized tests lined the walls. As I listened to Faith's professional concerns, desperation crept into her voice. I asked gentle questions to learn more about her life and her many positive qualities, just as Mr. Carson had done with me many years before. We talked about her vision for school counseling and the frustration she felt when she wasn't able to bring her ideas to fruition.

After Faith described her challenges and shared her feelings, I was ready to take action. I asked Faith to tell me the top three activities she wanted to incorporate into her program. I also offered several suggestions of my own. I then helped her outline a monthly calendar to ensure she had the time to implement these activities. Next, we discussed ways to convince Faith's principal that a comprehensive, data-driven school counseling program would not only benefit the students but support the principal's goals.

Being new, however, to the school and the profession, Faith didn't feel comfortable making requests of the principal. She needed help to present her case. As her mentor, I suggested we speak to the principal together. During our next few sessions, Faith and I focused on clarifying Faith's vision for her program, ensuring that each aspect of her plan was backed by sound reasoning and established best practices. We then developed an outline of the key points for our conversation with the principal.

Through practice and role play, I helped Faith express her ideas verbally. I provided positive feedback to boost her self-confidence and offered suggestions for improvement to assist her in refining her presentation.

Still, Faith was nervous. She feared she would either lose her job for appearing insubordinate or put a strain on her relationship with her principal by speaking up. I told her she was doing the right thing for her school community. She had valuable gifts to offer, and she had the ability to successfully advocate for her students and her profession.

After several additional sessions with Faith, she was ready for the conversation. I joined her and her principal in the school's conference room. We began as planned, asking the principal questions to better understand her vision for the school. We listened carefully and took notes on how a comprehensive school counseling program would help the principal accomplish each of her goals. Then we shared our school counseling plan, along with data and a needs assessment, as well as our ideas for implementing individual counseling, small group work, classroom lessons, school-wide initiatives, community initiatives, and a monthly calendar of activities.

The potential of this comprehensive plan clearly inspired the principal. The three of us spent the rest of the morning discussing how Faith's proposal could be implemented. The principal became an active participant in planning the program and removed several of the time-consuming responsibilities in Faith's way.

Faith needed advocacy and hands-on support to make changes at her school, given how her talents were not being fully utilized in service of her students. It's important to note here that, as we discussed in chapter 3, caring mentoring should lead to empowerment rather than dependency. In some cases, empowering mentees requires mentors to assist with a project or be the mentee's voice in order to help the mentee progress in their development. Mentees, however, should not become dependent on their mentor in the long term.

The key here is for the mentor to always keep in mind how their mentee can reach professional independence.

When mentees rely too much on their mentors, they lose the opportunity to develop important skills and the confidence that only comes with experience. In Faith's case, collaborating on a plan for communicating with her principal served to teach Faith how to perform these functions on her own in the future. This method also provided Faith with the support she needed to build her program and spend more time working with students.

On this occasion, caring mentoring produced a positive result for Faith. Circumstances, however, may not always take a favorable turn for our mentees, at least not immediately. Some principals may refuse to be flexible, and even when we have the best of intentions, our mentorship may not go as planned. Regardless of the outcome in a particular situation, a caring mentoring relationship builds essential skills, strengthens resolve to handle tough situations, and contributes to mentees' ongoing professional growth.

Create Leadership Opportunities for Your Mentees

During my first years teaching reading and peer counseling at the high school level, I was fortunate to receive action-oriented mentoring from Mrs. Lewis, one of the school's administrators. Mrs. Lewis was an energetic woman in her midforties who always looked toward a brighter future for our students and school community. Throughout our relationship, she encouraged me to get more involved at the school and eventually asked me to serve on the school's leadership team.

That request changed everything. I began to see how the school functioned as a whole instead of how I saw it through the limited viewpoint of my classroom. I also attended a leadership retreat and spent several days building relationships with the other members of the leadership team. Together, we crafted a vision for improving our school.

During the retreat, Mrs. Lewis assigned me several small leadership roles. I facilitated group discussions, chaired subcommittees, and shared information with the rest of the staff. As a result of these assignments, I realized I had something valuable to offer as a leader. I learned I could bring people together. I recognized the talents of others and inspired them to use their abilities to make our school a better place.

The following year, Mrs. Lewis tasked me with training our staff on professional development days. In this role, I developed the ability to work with people of different experience levels, backgrounds, and interests. Sometimes I had to encourage gently, and other times I had to motivate more vigorously. Through it all, I learned to become a leader in the school. I helped other teachers to grow while improving my own instructional practices.

In addition to challenging me to grow, Mrs. Lewis introduced me to other leaders within the school. Through the leadership team I met Marcella, a school counselor who worked with students in the Exceptional Student Education program, and we collaborated on several leadership initiatives during the school year.

These initiatives gave me the chance to observe Marcella in her work as a school counselor. She was kindhearted and knowledgeable, and everyone in the school respected her. I heard the love in Marcella's voice when she spoke to students, and I watched her build positive relationships with each young person who stepped into her office.

Marcella inspired me through her example of how a school counselor could support the success of students, even under the most difficult of circumstances. When I asked Marcella how she became a school counselor, she introduced me to the master's program in school counseling from which I eventually graduated.

My mentorship with Mrs. Lewis supported my professional development in two key ways. First, the challenges she offered me fostered my growth as an educator. Second, she put me in a position to network with others, which expanded my vision of what was possible in my role as a teacher. Before I met Mrs. Lewis, my professional development was limited to my experience in the classroom. Mrs. Lewis helped me discover qualities within myself that I had not known existed. Additionally, working in different capacities throughout the school gave me a better understanding of what it meant to be an educator. The people I met became instrumental to my growth as a leader.

When I train mentors in our district, I encourage them to look for appropriate ways for mentees to assume leadership roles. It's essential that these experiences are commensurate with mentees' abilities because the goal is to challenge them in ways that build confidence. Not all mentees will become school leaders, but when we challenge them by putting them in the position to contribute, we help them grow.

As we discussed in chapter 1, mentors should take note of their mentees' strengths and consider how they can use these abilities to be of service in their schools. Mentors should then arrange for their mentees to apply their strengths in ways that assist others. As mentees engage with their schools, they develop valuable skills and form key relationships with others that promote long-term success.

Equip Your Mentees with Valuable Information and Resources

Another way we as mentors act on behalf of our mentees is to offer them resources designed to support their professional success, growth, and well-being. This expresses our care and provides mentees with the information to help them develop further. Passing along relevant materials is a powerful action mentors take on behalf of their mentees. Olivia's story further illustrates this point.

I asked Olivia, an elementary school teacher who had been in our district for several years, if I could meet her in her classroom to talk about her experience as a new teacher mentee. When we sat down together, I invited her to share a time when she'd felt cared for within an educational mentoring relationship. A wide smile spread across Olivia's face. During her first year of teaching, her mentor, Mrs. Upton, collected every lesson plan, teaching checklist, and resource they had used and saved them.

At the end of the year, Mrs. Upton surprised Olivia with a flash drive containing all of the materials. This gift had a profound impact on Olivia. She laughed and told me she still uses these materials as a part of her teaching. "Mrs. Upton had been doing this for me all along," Olivia said, "and didn't even tell me about it. This gift took a lot of time on her part, and it showed me she really cared."

I nodded. Sensing Olivia's deep appreciation for Mrs. Upton, I wondered what else Mrs. Upton had done to mentor Olivia. When I asked for additional examples, Olivia's eyes moistened. One day, during the last month of her first year of teaching, Olivia was absent from school. Mrs. Upton went into her classroom and, with the help of the substitute teacher, asked each student to share what they had learned from Olivia. She recorded the students' comments on video.

Olivia's voice wavered as she described how grateful she felt when Mrs. Upton presented her with the video. To this day, the video reminds Olivia that teachers make a difference in every child's life whether they know it at the time or not. She added, "I look at that video and remember how far I've come and how much teaching means to me." By the time we finished our conversation, Olivia and I had both gained a deeper understanding of the power mentors have to support a mentee's well-being through meaningful resources and gifts.

Mrs. Upton expressed her care for Olivia by creating something that inspired Olivia. The flash drive became a valued resource for Olivia, aiding her ability to teach successfully in the future. The video served as an important reminder of the positive impact her teaching has on students' lives (note that filming students may require a release form signed by a parent or guardian).

Another way mentors take action on behalf of their mentees is by recommending or gifting books that support mentees' growth and success. I'll always remember two books that Mr. Carson, one of my mentors, gave to me: *Wooden: A Lifetime of Observations and Reflections On and Off the Court* by John Wooden and *Leading with the Heart: Coach K's Successful Strategies for Basketball, Business, and Life* by Mike Krzyzewski. Mr. Carson once told me that he saw in me the potential to be the kind of leader who changes lives. He thought I'd benefit from the principles outlined in both these books.

He was right. These books were exactly what I needed at the time. Mr. Carson recognized my love for sports, which informed his choice of books, both of which use basketball as a metaphor for life. From John Wooden's book, I learned the value of developing my own philosophy of teaching and counseling. He reaffirmed my belief in the importance of relationships, and from him I learned to focus on ongoing improvements rather than final results. Mike Krzyzewski's book taught me how to build teams through vision, structure, and unity while navigating the inevitable obstacles that arise along the way.

Thanks to Mr. Carson, recommending books to my mentees is a part of my mentoring tool kit. I keep a record of books that I have found meaningful, and I list many of these books in the Suggested Reading and Resources section.

In addition, I ask my mentees about the books they've read. This helps me determine what would be a good fit for them, plus this prevents me from recommending books my mentees have already read. Giving books to my mentees has proven to be a powerful exercise. Afterward, I schedule time to discuss the content, and my mentees and I have had many fruitful conversations about what they have learned and how the information can be applied.

Provide Hands-on Support and Protection for Your Mentees When Needed

I interviewed Felicia, a veteran elementary school teacher who is studying to become a school administrator, in the reading corner of her classroom. As I sat across from her at a small table, I asked Felicia what it meant to feel cared for in a mentoring relationship.

She shared that during her first year she gave an assignment that the parents of one of her students did not believe was developmentally appropriate. The next morning, the parent stormed into the school, furious that his child was asked to do this assignment. The parent demanded to see the curriculum. Felicia panicked. As a new teacher, she was afraid of losing her job. She didn't know what to do, so she excused herself from the conversation and called her mentor, Ms. Newhouse, for support. Ms. Newhouse stopped what she was doing, found the content standards, brought them to the office, and showed the parent that this exercise was indeed developmentally appropriate for the student. "Ms. Newhouse was right there to fight for me when I was scared."

Felicia touched her palms together in a gesture of gratitude. At that point in her career, she had never before encountered an upset parent, and his anger intimidated her. While she felt that she could handle this type of situation now, as a less experienced teacher she had been deeply grateful for Ms. Newhouse's protection and support.

Because Felicia and Ms. Newhouse had already built a relationship, Felicia felt comfortable reaching out during a vulnerable moment. Had Felicia not felt safe asking Ms. Newhouse for help when she needed it, the situation could easily have escalated. This story demonstrates how one of the ways in which a mentor can show their mentees they care is by providing protection when needed.

New teachers and school counselors often enter schools without the knowledge needed to navigate many of the inevitable challenges. Even outstanding new educators face situations they are not prepared to handle alone, simply because they have not yet gained the required experience. In these circumstances, mentors express care by standing up for their mentees during times of need. In Felicia's case, Ms. Newhouse provided emotional support by being available and taking the concrete action needed to resolve the conflict.

Help Your Mentees Gain a Sense of Belonging

Later in our conversation, Felicia described another way Ms. Newhouse aided her in her growth. Each Friday, some of the veteran teachers at her school held what they called a "bagel morning." Ms. Newhouse invited Felicia to join the more experienced teachers at these events as they discussed what was happening at the school and swapped stories about the events in their classrooms.

Felicia grinned as she described how these mornings helped her grow as a teacher, commenting, "Just by absorbing what they said." Felicia felt touched that Ms. Newhouse had brought her into the group. As a result, Felicia learned new ways of working with students and parents, plus she gained exposure to new lesson ideas and benefitted from the perspectives of other educators. Most important, perhaps, it was during those breakfast meetings that Felicia first started to feel that she belonged in her school.

In addition, Felicia noted that Ms. Newhouse always made a point to recognize her successful efforts in front of the group, commenting, "Ms. Newhouse would tell the other teachers and even administrators when I taught a good lesson or came up with a creative idea." Being acknowledged in this way helped Felicia establish credibility among her peers and sparked conversations that opened the door to collegial relationships she cherishes to this day.

Sensing Felicia had more to share, I asked her if she remembered any other examples of how Ms. Newhouse took action on her behalf. Felicia thought for a moment and then described how Ms. Newhouse had invited her to collaborate on their school's multicultural night, an experience which also helped Felicia establish an increased sense of belonging.

Felicia used her experience as a dancer to choreograph several dances from other cultures, and students performed these dances the evening of the event. These activities became a meaningful learning experience for all involved. As a result, other teachers and staff members had a chance to appreciate Felicia's skills and creativity firsthand, further helping her to emerge as a valued member of the school's team.

Another way Ms. Newhouse helped Felicia find a place within her school community was to invite Felicia to join her at school concerts and plays. Ms. Newhouse told Felicia that attending these events not only supported the school but offered her a valuable opportunity to learn more about her students and develop relationships with their families. As Ms. Newhouse introduced Felicia to the people she knew and encouraged Felicia to build her own connections, Felicia gained a sense of comfort and acceptance that helped her navigate her first year.

When Ms. Newhouse invited Felicia to breakfast meetings with other experienced teachers, she provided Felicia with access to a support network she would not have otherwise had. Interacting with successful teachers put Felicia in a position to learn from others, in addition to Ms. Newhouse, leading to greater insights into her craft. Ms. Newhouse knew Felicia wanted to be a lifelong educator and an active member of the school's community. She put Felicia, therefore. in situations where she formed lasting relationships with established colleagues.

Ms. Newhouse also made sure Felicia participated in school projects, allowing her to showcase her skills in front of her coworkers and administrators. These actions helped Felicia earn the respect of her colleagues, making her a valued member of the staff. Sometimes Ms. Newhouse supported Felicia by sharing positive stories about her teaching, and sometimes Ms. Newhouse partnered with Felicia on public projects so others could see Felicia's good work for themselves.

In addition to helping Felicia find a sense of belonging within the walls of her new school, Ms. Newhouse recognized the importance of establishing Felicia as a member of the community. By encouraging Felicia to attend school events and taking the time to join her, Ms. Newhouse opened the door to essential connections. As a result, Felicia learned more about her students' families, and the families had a chance to become better acquainted with their children's teacher. These relationships helped Felicia acclimate to her new environment and build the sense of safety and belonging she needed.

Suggestions for Acting on Behalf of Your Mentees

The following list outlines specific suggestions for applying Caring Mentor Practice #5 in the areas of advocating and providing protection for your mentees, creating leadership opportunities, equipping your mentees with valuable information and resources, and helping your mentees gain a sense of belonging within the school community.

Advocate and Provide Protection for Your Mentees

- Establish a trusting relationship that allows your mentees to reach out when they need help.

- Provide hands-on assistance to help your mentees solve their problems.

- Stand up for your mentees as needed. For example, when a difficult situation arises, schedule an appointment with an administrator and provide support by sitting in on the conversation.

- Always keep in mind that your goal is to help your mentees become independent, competent professionals.

Create Leadership Opportunities for Your Mentees

- Identify your mentees' unique talents through conversation and the strengths assessments discussed in chapter 1.

- Challenge your mentees to take on leadership roles that allow them to put their talents into action.

- Discuss mentees' leadership projects to help them learn from these experiences.

Equip Your Mentees with Valuable Information and Resources

- Share practical resources with your mentees, such as instructional materials and motivational reminders.

- Recommend books to support your mentees' growth.

- Discuss with your mentees what they learned from their reading.

Help Your Mentees Gain a Sense of Belonging

- Invite your mentees to be a part of school traditions.

- Recognize your mentees' positive qualities publicly.

- Collaborate with your mentees on school projects and initiatives.

- Attend school and community events with your mentees to assist them in making connections with others.

Bringing It All Together

New teachers and school counselors face many challenges during their first years in education. As caring mentors, we must take concrete actions to support our mentees' progress. By doing so, we help our mentees find their footing during times of uncertainty, as well as develop valuable skills and relationships.

We also remind our mentees they're not alone when they face the inevitable difficulties that come with their new positions. In chapter 6, we turn our attention to how to overcome some of the key barriers to effective care.

CHAPTER 6

Overcoming Barriers to Care
in the Mentoring Relationship

Mentors face many challenges as they strive to care for their mentees while helping them establish themselves as successful professionals. My experiences mentoring and supporting other mentors have taught me there are a few fundamental barriers to implementing the 5 Practices of the Caring Mentor. These challenges include mentees who are uncooperative or resistant to the mentoring process, insufficient time for mentoring, a lack of opportunities to receive training and support as a mentor, insufficient tools for self-monitoring and self-assessment, and the difficult emotions that may arise throughout the mentoring process. In this chapter, we explore these challenges and discuss solutions.

Working with Uncooperative or Resistant Mentees

Over the years, I've observed that most teacher and school counselor mentees are open, receptive, and willing to learn. In some cases, however, mentees resist the mentoring process. In fact, a common question I receive when training mentors is, "What does the practice of caring mentoring look like when mentees are uncooperative, difficult to reach, and unwilling to learn or receive our care?"

Once, at the start of the school year, I noticed that Tim, a broad-shouldered veteran counselor with gray hair and a goatee, was not attending our required school counseling meetings. In addition, he had failed to complete the standard tasks we ask of counselors during the first few weeks of school. As a result, I received an email from his school administrator expressing concern about his attitude and performance. When I called Tim to discuss the situation, he said he had his program under control and didn't need to be told what to do. After spending several minutes reassuring Tim my intention was to support him rather than to direct him, he agreed to meet with me.

Tim had transferred from another school district. Now near retirement, he was much older than I was and had many more years of experience. When we finally sat down in Tim's office, I immediately sensed that he was not happy about being mentored. He quickly confirmed this through his actions. He shuffled his papers while I spoke and seldom made eye contact. We didn't accomplish much during that first meeting. I decided, therefore, to take some time to regroup, and I scheduled a follow-up meeting a week later.

In the days leading up to our next meeting, I wondered if there was something I had said or done to offend Tim, or if I lacked something as a mentor that precipitated his behavior. As I drove to our meeting, I had butterflies in my stomach. When we sat down for the second time in Tim's office, I told him that I understood he was an experienced counselor who was not looking to be mentored. I asked him how he wanted to proceed.

The lines on Tim's forehead deepened as he spoke about his extensive knowledge of school counseling and expressed his frustration at having to review information he felt he had already mastered. As I listened carefully, I realized I needed to approach my mentorship of Tim in a way that aligned with the adult learning principles we discussed in chapter 2.

With this in mind, I asked Tim to tell me what he thought was working well in his program and to share some of the specific challenges he was experiencing. As he spoke, I focused on listening with an open mind, intent on understanding his perspective. By honoring Tim's wealth of experience, I showed him respect. I made sure everything we discussed was directly related to the problems he was facing.

I then invited Tim to collaborate with me on developing a personalized plan for our mentoring activities. I still insisted, of course, that Tim attend our mandatory meetings and complete the required tasks, but this collaborative approach, which included his input on the content of our mentoring sessions, gave him a greater sense of control and self-determination.

As time passed, the lines on Tim's forehead softened, and he opened up about the difficulties of working in a new school environment. I realized, as I got to know Tim better, that he was a critical thinker by nature. In order to connect with him, I needed to present information in terms of problems and solutions rather than using the more inspirational approach that often worked well with other counselors. After making this adjustment, Tim expressed some willingness to receive assistance as he developed a weekly schedule for providing school counseling lessons to every classroom. We were now making progress, and after a few more sessions, Tim began to cooperate.

My experience with Tim provided me with several key insights that have helped me work more effectively with mentees who are resistant to the mentoring process. When I first encountered resistance from Tim, I took his behavior personally. I felt angry and doubted my own abilities. I needed to become aware of these emotions and learn not to react to them before I could resolve to not take Tim's actions personally. When my emotions intensified, I tuned in to my breathing and shifted my attention away from myself and toward serving Tim and his needs. Tim faced many challenges coming into a new school and initially felt that I, a mentor who was much younger than him, was not taking his life experiences into account. By empathizing with him, I changed that perception.

As a result of our strengthened connection, I was able to be more objective in my relationship with Tim. Some of the points he made were, in fact, true and assisted me in being a better mentor. I also focused on what Tim was doing right, such as thinking critically about his work, and proceeded to build on his assets rather than placing my attention solely on what I felt he was doing wrong.

Instead of labeling Tim as "difficult" and relating to him from that perspective, I needed to identify the specific behaviors that seemed problematic and develop a plan for addressing them. In Tim's case, he believed he already knew the content I was attempting to teach him. I therefore invited him to tell me what he wanted to learn, and we collaborated on a plan to make our mentoring activities more relevant to his specific needs.

Although I remained flexible with Tim, I also maintained consistency by insisting that he attend mandatory meetings and complete his assigned tasks. On rare occasions a mentee may remain uncooperative even after assistance or corrective action has taken place. When this happens, mentors should reach out to the administration for support.

In this case, Tim eventually came around. I arranged for make-up sessions so he could catch up on the meetings he had missed, and he made good progress in building a successful counseling program at his school. I am grateful for what Tim taught me. As a result of working with him, I've learned to make a distinction between how I approach mentoring new counselors and how I approach mentoring experienced counselors who, though new to the district, are already well versed in their craft.

Overcoming the Challenge of Insufficient Time

When learning the 5 Practices of the Caring Mentor for the first time, mentors often ask, "How will I have time to put these ideas into action?" When left unchecked, demanding workloads prevent mentors from meeting with mentees frequently enough to make a lasting impact. Additionally, their packed schedules often leave mentors feeling pressured, which leads them to rush through mentoring interactions rather than taking the time needed to effectively express their care.

Lindsey, a middle-aged eleventh grade English teacher, was mentoring a new teacher at her high school. When we sat down in the training room after a workshop, she shared some of the challenges she'd had in her mentoring practice during the first semester. Lindsey explained that teaching classes, grading papers, and fulfilling her responsibilities as a member of her school's leadership team seemed to make it impossible to give her mentee the necessary time. She understood the value of care but felt that her other work responsibilities and the subsequent lack of time formed a significant obstacle in her relationship with her mentee.

We started by reviewing Lindsey's schedule. Her school used a traditional block format, consisting of four ninety-minute classes per day, which each took place over the course of one semester. Lindsey's typical day started early. She prepped in her classroom, taught first period, had planning second period, ate lunch, then taught classes during third and fourth periods. After school, Lindsey reorganized her classroom before grading papers, planning with other teachers, and attending to her leadership team responsibilities. I asked Lindsey to write all this down in detail, allowing us to view her schedule as a whole. We then did the same for her mentee's schedule.

When we placed the schedules side by side, we had a clear vision of how Lindsey and her mentee were spending their days. We searched for periods of free time Lindsey could devote to mentoring. This process showed the time limitations Lindsey and her mentee were struggling with, but it also made the times they were both available more apparent. With their current schedules, the only feasible times for Lindsey and her mentee to meet were before school, during lunch, and after school.

I then asked Lindsey to help me brainstorm solutions, which we wrote down and discussed. Our task was to develop a mentoring schedule that allowed Lindsey to accomplish her own work while still providing sufficient time to serve as a caring mentor. As the ideas started to flow, we identified three periods of time Lindsey could devote to mentoring without compromising her other responsibilities. Lindsey decided to invite her mentee to come to her classroom before school one day a week, to have lunch with her every Friday, and to grade papers together one afternoon a week.

This new schedule gave Lindsey more time to speak informally with her mentee and also allowed them to combine their mentoring activities with work tasks such as planning and grading papers. In addition, I suggested Lindsey request that her administration schedule a common planning period for her and her mentee during the next semester. Lindsey agreed and also decided to ask for a substitute teacher one day per quarter to give her time to observe her mentee in the classroom. Lindsey's administration granted these requests, which resulted in additional time for observation, feedback, collaboration, and extended mentoring conversations.

Another challenge Lindsay faced was that she felt rushed during her mentoring sessions. She had a lot of content to share with her mentee but didn't want to sacrifice her commitment to care by rushing through their time together. I encouraged Lindsay to identify two or three points to focus on during a single mentoring session instead of attempting to address all her mentee's needs at once. For example, rather than trying to cover everything needed to get organized before a new semester, Lindsay concentrated on helping her mentee analyze her students' academic data and develop lesson plans to meet their specific needs. This allowed Lindsay to slow down and give each subject the needed time and attention without feeling pressured to fit too much into each session.

Thriving as a caring mentor takes a wholehearted effort to ensure that sufficient time is available for mentoring. For these relationships to flourish, mentors must take practical actions, including analyzing their and their mentees' schedules, cooperating with the administration, and setting aside the necessary time for meaningful interactions.

Lindsey was able to overcome these difficulties by finding time to serve as a caring mentor while honoring her own professional needs. To accomplish this, she analyzed her daily schedule, blended mentoring and work activities, sought administrative support, kept her mentoring sessions focused, and reflected on her progress.

Being a caring mentor was clearly a priority for Lindsay. Her actions, including her determined attitude and the personal value she placed on care, demonstrated a high degree of dedication to her role as a mentor. Lindsey's commitment to implementing the 5 Practices of the Caring Mentor led her to think deeply about how she could reorganize her mentoring time and take practical steps to maximize her efficiency. Her mentee consequently received the benefits of caring mentoring support, which not only contributed to her well-being and enhanced professional practice but also made a positive impact on her students.

Insufficient Mentor Training, Feedback, and Support

Most professional development made available for teachers and school counselors is related to instructional and counseling practices. Little training, however, is directed toward the process of mentoring itself and helping mentors express care in support of their mentees. This leaves many mentors feeling supported in their work in the classroom or the counseling office but unsupported in their roles as mentors.

The solutions to these challenges lie in the provision of mentor training and specific support in the practice of care as the foundation for mentoring. Being an effective, caring mentor requires instruction, practice, reflection, support, and feedback. One of the ways to fulfill these needs is to set up training sessions in which the principles of caring mentoring are taught, discussed, and practiced in preparation for mentors to apply these principles to their work with mentees. Trainers should follow up on these sessions with biweekly or monthly check-in calls to allow mentors to reflect on their mentoring practice, ask questions, and receive ongoing support as they work with their mentees throughout the school year.

When this kind of training is not available, consider forming a caring mentor support group. These groups, which may also supplement the training approaches described above, serve to provide mentors with the feedback and support they need to succeed. Sylvia, an outstanding school counselor and new mentor, was working with Xavier, a new counselor who had just graduated from college and had moved into our area from another state. Sylvia wanted to express care in her mentoring relationship with Xavier but struggled with finding the time to meet and helping him feel comfortable in his new environment.

Sylvia called me one Saturday afternoon to ask for advice. She wondered what other school counselor mentors were doing to help their mentees succeed despite their busy schedules. To help Sylvia answer this question, I arranged for a group of experienced mentors to meet after our next professional development session and invited Sylvia to join us. This group consisted of five mentors, including myself. We settled into a quiet corner of the training room and discussed the challenges we had encountered as we strove to put care first in our mentoring relationships. Together, we shared some best practices.

After this initial conversation, which we all found helpful, we decided to meet regularly. In addition, our group communicated via text whenever we were not able to gather in person. The counselors who participated in this group shared common challenges. For example, one member asked, "Is anyone else swamped with work? When are you finding time to focus on your mentees?" The group responded with reassurances, helpful suggestions, and lessons learned.

On another occasion, a mentor shared, "I started inviting my mentee into my classroom for a quick cup of coffee before school on Fridays. We've made it a tradition, and now we have a regular time to check in each week." Conversations such as these continued throughout the school year, and the group reported feeling a sense of mutual support as they benefited from the collective wisdom of their colleagues.

A caring mentor support group is a professional learning community in which participants have a safe place to share knowledge and experience, receive emotional support, and offer advice to improve the practice of care in their mentoring relationships. I recommend that such groups consist of four to eight mentors who meet regularly, whether formally or informally, to discuss and improve their implementation of the 5 Practices of the Caring Mentor.

These meetings, which may take place in person or through the use of texting, email, or video conferencing, give participants the opportunity to speak candidly and confidentially about their mentoring experiences and the difficulties they have encountered. Through these groups members receive valuable support and benefit from the group's collective input. Here are some possible questions to use in your discussions:

- What are some of the barriers you face when implementing the 5 Practices?

- How do you feel when these barriers arise?

- Is a mentee ever particularly difficult to reach during a mentoring session?

- Do you ever feel frustrated, angry, or overwhelmed during your mentoring experiences?

- Do you ever face systemic barriers such as struggling to find time or managing a heavy workload while trying to be a caring mentor?

- If so, what solutions work best for you?

The role of a support group is to help mentors better understand their experiences and work through the many challenges that arise while mentoring during a busy school year. Having a chance to express and process these difficult experiences can make the difference between an unsuccessful mentoring relationship and one that is both impactful for the mentee and fulfilling for the mentor.

Caring mentor support groups may be facilitated, when possible, by a school leader or mentoring coordinator. Or they may be run solely by the mentors themselves. The agenda for a group meeting should include a period of time to connect with one another, followed by timed segments that allow mentors to share their experiences, identify challenges, develop solutions, reflect on their mentoring practice, and look for opportunities to improve. I suggest keeping meetings under one hour in duration so that group members can consistently fit them into their schedules. A caring mentor support group serves as a safe container to hold the thoughts, emotions, challenges, and successes of mentors as they support one another in mentoring with care.

The purpose of caring mentor support groups is not to add another task to an already filled to-do list but rather to create meeting opportunities that are easy for mentors to plan and maintain. When mentors support one another, they are better able to make sense of the difficulties they face throughout the mentoring process. They also develop greater self-awareness as they learn from other mentors' approaches to care and have the opportunity to share their frustrations and successes. Together, mentors offer their best practices, learn from the best practices of others, renew their enthusiasm about serving as a caring mentor, and build relationships with other mentors as they provide each other emotional support.

Insufficient Tools for Self-Monitoring and Self-Assessment

As mentors strive to infuse their mentoring relationships with care by applying the 5 Practices of the Caring Mentor, they often lose focus and struggle to remember each of the practices. Mentors need a method to reflect on the degree to which they've applied the 5 Practices in their mentoring sessions. Concrete tools allow mentors to review their progress and thrive in their work.

To address these challenges, I recommend mentors use the Caring Mentor Checklist and the Caring Mentor Monthly Self-Assessment Form before and after each mentoring session. The checklist helps mentors reflect on the 5 Practices before their mentoring sessions and recommit to applying each of the practices. After the session, mentors use the Caring Mentor Monthly Self-Assessment Form to examine the degree to which they incorporated the 5 Practices.

The Caring Mentor Checklist

Prior to your mentoring session, I encourage you to review the 5 Practices of the Caring Mentor. You may decide to focus on one practice per session, or you may prefer to review all of them at once. After you read the practices and the accompanying reminders, set your intention to apply each of the practices with your mentee. This exercise helps you infuse your mentoring relationship with care by including each of the 5 Practices in your work.

Caring Mentor Practice #1: Caring mentors practice active listening to make a sincere connection with their mentees.

- Express sincere curiosity as you engage with your mentees.

- Listen with your full attention.

- Keep your facial expressions and body language warm and welcoming.

- Ask thoughtful and open-ended questions.

- Reflect what your mentees say back to them to check for understanding.

- Take time to consider and better understand your mentees' cultures.

- Focus on identifying your mentees' strengths and help them to express these strengths.

- Practice mindfulness as you work with your mentees.

Caring Mentor Practice #2: Caring mentors create a safe place for authentic expression.

- Make yourself available for your mentees both formally and informally.

- Discuss the meaning and importance of trust with your mentees.

- Respect your mentees as equal adults.

- Encourage your mentees to express themselves authentically.

- Validate your mentees' feelings.

- Remain nonjudgmental.

- Honor confidentiality.

- Recognize your mentees' positive qualities and share them with your mentees.

- Stay open to learning from your mentees.

Caring Mentor Practice #3: Caring mentors devote themselves to their mentees' growth.

- Ask your mentees thoughtful questions to encourage professional self-reflection.

- Identify your mentees' strengths and areas in need of improvement.

- Help your mentees build on their strengths and improve in the needed areas.

- Encourage your mentees to set meaningful daily and weekly goals.

- Set up weekly times to observe your mentees and provide constructive feedback.

- Instruct your mentees on the fundamentals needed to succeed in their positions.

- Collaborate with your mentees on projects to provide experience-based learning opportunities.

- Support your mentees as they move toward increased autonomy and independence.

- Live out what it means to be a lifelong learner as an example for your mentees.

Caring Mentor Practice #4: Caring mentors share their perspectives and insights with their mentees.

- Help your mentees identify and reflect on their why.

- Share your why with your mentees.

- Help your mentees explore and express their professional values.

- Offer your mentees perspectives and insights about ongoing learning, the value of making mistakes, and the way improvement unfolds over time.

- Encourage your mentees to recognize, reflect on, and celebrate their successes.

- Assure your mentees that experiencing a wide range of emotions during the first year in their profession is natural.

- Share some of your own professional challenges with your mentees and the ways in which you learned from them.

Caring Mentor Practice #5: Caring mentors act on behalf of their mentees.

- Advocate for your mentees' rights when needed.

- Provide hands-on assistance to your mentees.

- Connect your mentees with growth-enhancing experiences and leadership roles.

- Share resources with your mentees, including instructional and motivational materials.

- Introduce your mentees to colleagues and invite them to participate in school activities.

- Recognize your mentees' successes publicly.

The Caring Mentor Monthly Self-Assessment Form

The following self-assessment form is designed to assist you, after your mentoring sessions, in monitoring your use of the 5 Practices of the Caring Mentor. Record the date and, in each column, rate the degree to which you incorporated the indicated practice into your work with your mentee, using a separate row for each meeting.

At the end of the row, calculate your combined score for the session. Compare and contrast your scores across sessions for the month to identify the practices you implement successfully and the areas in need of improvement.

On the next pages are examples of blank and completed forms.

The Caring Mentor Monthly Self-Assessment Form

Blank Form

Mentor's Name: _____

Month/Year of Assessment: _____

Rating Scale

0 – I did not implement the practice in today's session.

1 – I implemented the practice minimally in today's session.

2 – I implemented the practice moderately in today's session.

3 – I implemented the practice thoroughly in today's session.

Session #	Date	Caring Mentor Practice #1 Score	Caring Mentor Practice #2 Score	Caring Mentor Practice #3 Score	Caring Mentor Practice #4 Score	Caring Mentor Practice #5 Score	Overall Score

The Caring Mentor Monthly Self-Assessment Form

Completed Example

Mentor's Name: Samuel Thomas

Month/Year of Assessment: January 2019

Rating Scale

0 – I did not implement the practice in today's session.

1 – I implemented the practice minimally in today's session.

2 – I implemented the practice moderately in today's session.

3 – I implemented the practice thoroughly in today's session.

Session #	Date	Caring Mentor Practice #1 Score	Caring Mentor Practice #2 Score	Caring Mentor Practice #3 Score	Caring Mentor Practice #4 Score	Caring Mentor Practice #5 Score	Overall Score
1	1/1/19	2	2	2	1	1	8
2	1/8/19	2	2	3	1	1	9
3	1/15/19	3	3	3	2	2	13
4	1/22/19	3	3	3	3	2	14
5	1/29/19	3	3	3	3	3	15

Analyzing the Caring Mentor Monthly Self-Assessment Form

As we see, Samuel recorded his lowest scores during the first week in January. By reflecting on his efforts and making adjustments, he increased his score on Caring Mentor Practice #3 the next week. By the third week, Samuel elevated his scores in other areas, and by tracking the degree to which he applied each practice and focusing on improving the needed areas, he implemented each practice thoroughly by the end of the month.

Working Through Our Own Difficult Emotions

Another key barrier to care arises when we are struggling with our own emotions. Even mentors with a deep commitment to care are still human beings with our own needs who experience emotional ups and downs. When I speak to mentors about working through our own emotions, especially when we feel overwhelmed, I share with them the Caring Mentor Emotional Regulation Process.

The Caring Mentor Emotional Regulation Process

1. Step Away Temporarily If Possible

   Stepping away refers to removing ourselves, when possible and appropriate, from a difficult situation so we may attend to our own needs. This gives us the time and space needed to gather our thoughts and determine a helpful response to the situation.

2. Identify the Emotion

   Identifying the emotion helps us gain perspective. Whether we're feeling anger, frustration, sadness, or something else, once we name a feeling our felt experience becomes clearer and less overwhelming. Labeling the emotion diminishes its power, allowing us to deal with it more consciously.

3. Feel the Emotion

   Next, take a few moments to feel the emotion. Explore your physical sensations as an objective observer. Mentors often push the emotion away or try to cover it up by engaging in more activities, allowing the emotion to fester. This is where stepping away becomes helpful. There will be times during our mentorship, however, when we will not have the opportunity to step away. In these cases, we should take time to feel the emotion as soon as we have a moment to ourselves.

4. Breathe through the Emotion

   Once you identify and feel the emotion, breathe through it. Allow the emotion to be just as it is, and then breathe slowly and evenly. Breathing oxygenates the brain and relaxes the body. Five slow, deep breaths are usually enough to help mentors calm their emotions and prepare them to return to productive activity.

Three Caring Mentor Questions for Responding to Challenges
After mentors use the steps above to work through difficult emotions and are ready to respond to the current obstacle, I advise them to reflect upon the following questions:

1. *What would someone who has compassion for himself or herself do?*

   Asking ourselves this question ensures that our next actions will be caring and respectful to ourselves, which usually leads to caring and respectful actions toward others. We can only care effectively for others when our own needs are met. Restoring our sense of well-being allows us to reconnect with the inner resources needed to extend care toward our mentees.

2. *Which of the 5 Practices of the Caring Mentor could I apply to care for my mentee in this moment?*

   Once we meet our own needs and treat ourselves with compassion, the next step is to consider how we can best care for our mentees. I ask mentors at this time to review the 5 Practices and decide which would be most helpful in the current circumstances. I then encourage them to apply the chosen practice as an expression of care toward their mentees.

3. *Am I ready to start over?*

    I've felt many times in my own mentoring journey that I've fallen short in my attempts to care effectively. I've learned, however, that we always have the opportunity to start over before we take the next positive step. When I ask myself, *Am I ready to start over?* I remember that each moment is new and that it offers me an opportunity to redirect my course toward caring for myself and others. When I start over, I reframe the situation by asking myself:

    - *What have I learned from this experience?*
    - *How has it helped me to become a better mentor?*
    - *What is the next positive step I can take in this moment?*

I then forgive myself, remembering that I'm human and often make mistakes, and I refocus my attention on implementing the 5 Practices to the best of my ability.

Suggestions for Overcoming the Barriers to Care

The following list outlines specific suggestions for overcoming the barriers to care in the areas of working with uncooperative or resistant mentees, overcoming the challenge of insufficient time, dealing with insufficient training and support, handling a lack of tools for self-assessment and self-monitoring, and working through one's own difficult emotions.

Working with Uncooperative or Resistant Mentees

- Remember that a mentee's challenging behavior is not personal. Focus on helping your mentee take the next step forward.

- Keep your emotions in check by analyzing your own thinking and practicing self-awareness.

- Work to understand your mentees' points of view and empathize with their feelings.

- Rather than labeling your mentees as "difficult," identify specific problematic behaviors and develop a plan of action to address each one.

- Focus on what your mentees are doing well and build upon their strengths.

- Take into account your mentees' personalities and communicate in ways that best meet their needs.

- Remain flexible while enforcing appropriate boundaries and insisting your mentees follow mandatory rules and procedures.

- Learn from your experiences with "difficult" mentees and use these to become a better mentor.

Overcoming the Challenge of Insufficient Time

- Write out and review both your schedule and your mentees' schedules to gain a clear sense of how everyone is using their time.

- Compare your schedules and look for times you are both available. Devote these times to mentoring.

- Brainstorm potential solutions with your mentees as you seek additional time for mentoring activities.

- Schedule regular meeting times based on common availability. These should be more formal meetings as opposed to the informal weekly check-ins recommended in chapter 1.

- Request administrative support. For example, ask for common planning times and schedule adjustments.

Insufficient Training, Reflection, Feedback, and Support

- Create a caring mentor support group for the opportunity to meet regularly with other mentors and share knowledge, experience, emotional support, and advice.

- Meet in person when possible or use texts, email, or social media.

- Create a safe environment in which group members may speak candidly, knowing conversations will remain confidential.

- Devote group meeting time to each of the following: connecting personally, sharing experiences, identifying challenges, developing solutions, setting goals, reflecting, and sharing best practices.

Insufficient Tools for Self-Monitoring and Self-Assessment

- Use the Caring Mentor Checklist to review the 5 Practices of the Caring Mentor and prepare yourself for a mentoring session.

- Use the Caring Mentor Monthly Self-Assessment Form to rate yourself on how well you apply the 5 Practices. Track your progress over time.

- Reflect regularly on your practice as a caring mentor.

Working Through Our Own Difficult Emotions

- Step away when possible.

- Identify the emotion.

- Feel the emotion.

- Breathe through the emotion.

- Ask *What would someone who has compassion for him or herself do in this moment?*

- Ask *How can I care for the person in front of me, and which of the 5 Practices can I apply in this moment?*

- Ask *Am I ready to start over?*

Bringing It All Together

In this chapter, we discussed some of the obstacles that arise as we navigate our mentoring relationships. Understanding these obstacles and applying the solutions above helps us maintain a caring perspective as we work to transform difficult situations into growth experiences.

Now that we've explored the key challenges of implementing the 5 Practices of the Caring Mentor and identified solutions, it's time to focus on caring for mentees during times of crisis. In the next chapter, we discuss serving as a caring mentor during a tragedy and explore approaches to guide our mentoring practice when mentees are going through a trauma that affects them both personally and professionally.

CHAPTER 7

Caring for Mentees
in Times of Crisis

During the time I was writing this book, an unimaginable tragedy occurred within our school community. On February 14th, 2018, I was at a district meeting when one of the department directors received an urgent phone call.

"We have a shooter in a school," he said.

That simple statement left all of us breathless.

As the details came in, we learned that a shooting had taken place at Marjory Stoneman Douglas High School, killing fourteen children and three staff members. In that moment, everything changed. The suffering within our community was overwhelming. Agendas that had previously seemed important faded into the background. The only things that mattered were keeping our students safe and supporting the victims and their families.

This devastating event severely impacted our entire community. Our district organized safety and support efforts, and I was assigned to assist at the elementary schools where students and staff were most affected, including schools where I already served as a mentor to several school counselors. Many of the students, family members, and staff at those schools had close connections to both those killed and those who had survived, several of whom were seriously injured.

Over the following weeks, as a small part of the much greater efforts provided by our district team, I visited each of the schools, working with my school counselor mentees to support everyone in our community as they processed their fear, trauma, and grief during this unspeakably difficult time.

Collaborative Planning and Action

In the first days after the shooting, the priority of staff and other district personnel was to address the immediate needs of the school community. As such, caring mentoring took the form of collaborative planning with my mentees to ensure everyone's physical and psychological safety. We wrote out a list of the school's needs and developed plans to meet those needs. We implemented our plans by taking the following actions:

- Before school, we contributed to key safety efforts, such as ensuring all adults on campus were visible, engaged, and welcoming as students and families arrived.

- We briefed teachers, based on guidelines provided by district leadership, on how to speak to students about the tragedy in sensitive, compassionate, and developmentally appropriate ways.

- We encouraged teachers and administrators to maintain a consistent routine and to reassure students of their safety.

- Together with the student and psychological services departments, we organized mental health teams and placed them within schools to connect them with individuals in need of emotional support.

- We urged staff to identify students, colleagues, and other members of the community who were in distress. We put those individuals in touch with the front office staff so they would receive immediate assistance.

- We listened deeply, offering many hugs, to all the students, staff members, and families affected.

In addition to these activities, we met with staff after school, offering time and space for everyone to embrace and support each other. My mentees and I spoke to groups about connecting to our common purpose, which in that moment meant working together in our efforts to support our school communities and each other. We regularly discussed the challenges that arose and collaborated on solutions. We reached out to school families to learn about and meet their specific needs.

We also knew that students, families, and staff needed ongoing grief and trauma support. Caring for them therefore meant assisting my mentees by working with district staff to bring in additional resources. As a part of our district's support plan, we communicated with leaders from other departments to coordinate the services of social workers, school psychologists, and family counselors. We also brought in local teams of therapy dogs, who helped calm students and staff.

Emotional Support

We all worked tirelessly to meet the immediate needs of the school community, which meant some of my mentees needed emotional support themselves. My mentees worked for long periods with few breaks, which led to a combination of physical fatigue and secondary traumatic stress. I cared for my mentees by listening deeply and offering them my full attention, assuring them that I was there to support them. In a crisis, the quality of our attentiveness and our willingness to be present during the other person's trauma and grief often brings more comfort and healing than the specific words we say.

One of my mentees had close connections to some of the victims. One afternoon, as we sat in his office, he shared that he had been so focused on helping others that he hadn't had time to feel his own emotions. With a heavy heart, he showed me photographs of a victim he had known well and told me how that person had impacted his life. His tears flowed, and I embraced him, giving him a compassionate space in which to grieve. I could not take away his sorrow, but I could share it.

My mentee needed validation. He needed to know that what he was experiencing was okay and that he would be supported unconditionally as he worked through his feelings. Through my facial expressions, body language, tone of voice, and gentle questions, I showed him the deep respect I had for him and his grief.

He also needed a voice in his own healing process, and so I asked how I could best support him.

He replied, "Just being here, listening, and talking with me is what I need right now."

I told my mentee that I cared about him unconditionally as a human being, not just because he was suffering through this tragedy. I expressed this, when the time was right, by asking him about other aspects of his life. This helped him gain perspective and understand that I saw him as a whole person who, though he had experienced grief and trauma, was not defined by these emotions.

I also gave my mentee the contact information of our district's Employee Assistance Program, which provides access to trained trauma specialists. Once my mentee expressed some of the intense emotions he had been carrying inside of him, he began to feel somewhat better. Knowing that the healing process contains many ups and downs, I encouraged him to keep my phone number close by and reach out whenever he needed me.

Immediately following this tragedy, caring mentoring was best expressed through concrete action, as described in chapter 5. Along with the rest of our district team, I needed to focus my efforts on providing safety and emotional support to everyone involved before any other mentoring work could be effective. As a district, we collaborated on a clear plan, communicated with school community members, and gathered additional resources and support.

Dealing with a tragedy of this magnitude is not only difficult for students and families but also for the caregivers. My mentees needed different degrees of emotional support themselves once the immediate needs of the situation were met. Some mentees simply needed a safe place to share their thoughts and feelings, while others needed deeper levels of ongoing, trauma-informed support.

It's important to note here that it is not ethical for a mentor to take on the sole responsibility of providing crisis counseling for mentees, unless the mentor is trained in this area and has been appointed to serve this function. When mentees experience severe trauma, the mentor should refer them to a licensed professional, which is why I referred my mentees to our district's Employee Assistance Program.

Trauma-Informed Mentoring

Mentors should, however, possess an understanding of trauma-informed methods for when they do find themselves working with mentees who have endured a crisis. I had attended several trainings on trauma-informed approaches, and so I knew my mentees might be worried about their safety and the safety of others. It would not be unusual for them to feel fear or anxiety. Some mentees, in fact, might withdraw or express a wide range of other coping behaviors as they dealt with their feelings.

Understanding this, I worked with my mentees using the strategies I had learned from my research and training. As discussed in previous chapters, I created a safe place for mentees to express themselves while I listened deeply and helped them make sense of their experiences. It's important to remember that every person deals with crisis differently. We as mentors must therefore be attentive and responsive to our mentees' unique needs.

Flexibility

I remained flexible in my approach, providing my mentees with a sense of control and empowerment within our interactions. I asked gentle questions and stayed focused on providing unconditional warmth and acceptance to my mentees rather than always trying to say the perfect thing. I practiced open awareness, placing my full attention on my mentees with a welcoming and nonjudgmental attitude. I also let mentees share at their own pace, asking follow-up questions when they seemed ready to say more. Sometimes we simply sat in silence, which gave my mentees time to process their emotions.

Supporting Others and Taking Care of Ourselves

Later, I interviewed an experienced mentor who worked with a new teacher in the area where the tragedy had taken place. We walked through a nearby park after school, and she shared how, in her view, mentoring during a time of crisis requires two points of emphasis. She needed to help her mentee support her students as they worked through their trauma, and she needed to assist her mentee in dealing with her own complex feelings in the aftermath of the event.

The teacher she was mentoring reported that her students all had different ways of dealing with the experience. Some students appeared outwardly sad or angry, while others seemed stunned or dazed. Some students needed to talk, while others preferred to be left alone.

Caring mentoring took the form of encouraging the teacher to follow the district's suggestions of maintaining an environment of minimal academic pressure as she supported her students' recovery. She incorporated several calming activities into her classroom routine, such as sculpting with clay, putting puzzles together, and working as a class in the school garden. The teacher spoke to her students in a soothing tone of voice while remaining sensitive to the short- and long-term impact her words might have.

Scheduling Times to Check In and Talk

The mentor I interviewed made sure to set aside time to check in and allow her mentee to express whatever was on her mind. During one of these chats, the teacher shared her concerns about the students who didn't seem to be outwardly affected by the tragedy. She wanted to make sure these students also received the help they needed.

Her mentor advised her to contact the school counseling department. Over time, however, it became apparent that the teacher's concern for her students reflected her own need for support. Eventually, the teacher opened up about the stress she was feeling, and her mentor encouraged her to seek a professional counselor. The mentor, meanwhile, continued to make herself available to listen and offer whatever practical or emotional support she could.

Stages of Trauma Recovery

Recovering from trauma takes time and involves several stages. Mentors should be mindful to offer their caring support throughout each part of this process. Mentors must understand how some of the common effects of trauma unfold in different ways at different times. These effects include struggling with powerful emotions such as anger or sadness, exhibiting aggressive tendencies, disassociating, or allowing oneself to become numb to avoid the pain. We support our mentees best when we approach our mentoring relative to the stage of trauma they're going through at a given point in time. The Suggested Reading and Resources section at the end of this book lists resources that discuss these stages and how to work with people in trauma.

Enlisting the Help of a Trained Specialist

Again, it is important to note that teacher and school counselor mentors should not take sole responsibility for helping their mentees recover from trauma. Trauma counseling should be provided by trained specialists, and mentors should encourage mentees in trauma to seek support from licensed professionals. Mentors must understand, however, how to implement trauma-informed approaches when mentoring those who have recently experienced a crisis.

Suggestions for Caring for Mentees in Times of Crisis

The following list outlines specific suggestions for caring for mentees in times of crisis.

- Address mentees' immediate needs first.

- Develop short- and long-term plans to help mentees work through their trauma.

- Allow mentees to process their experiences in their own ways and to share at their own pace.

- Apply trauma-informed approaches when working with your mentees.

- Provide trauma-informed guidance to assist your mentees in working with their students and school communities.

- Check in with your mentees regularly and offer consistent support.

- Connect your mentees and their school communities with the appropriate mental health professionals.

Bringing It All Together

Our journeys as caring mentors often take unexpected turns. Sometimes these appear as minor bumps in the road, while at other times they are life-changing events or tragedies. We cannot separate our mentoring from life itself. Life rarely unfolds as planned, and there is a real possibility that events which we never could have imagined may occur.

We may need to bear down and apply a certain degree of toughness and grit to help our mentees through certain situations. Other occasions require tenderness, compassion, and patience. We must always remember, however, that although our mentees are professionals who participate in the mentoring process to improve themselves as educators, they are first and foremost human beings who deserve our kindness, respect, and care—especially when dealing with trauma.

CHAPTER 8

The Importance of
Self-Care for Mentors

C aring mentors must also recognize the importance of self-care. Self-care refers to the actions we purposefully take to enhance our physical, social, emotional, and psychological well-being. Serving as a caring mentor requires a great deal of energy and focus on other people to be effective. If we neglect to care for ourselves, however, we ignore the value of care as it applies to our own lives, and we diminish our capacity to care for others.

When I feel overwhelmed as a result of extended periods of caring for mentees, I ask myself the first of the Three Caring Mentor Questions for Responding to Challenges discussed in chapter 6.: *What would a mentor who has compassion for himself do in this situation?* This reminds me that I am a human being who also has needs and helps me take care of myself as I care for others.

When I want to encourage mentors to practice self-care, I ask them to imagine a precious person in their lives and to hold the image of that person lovingly in their mind's eye. Then I ask the following questions:

- Would you ask this person to perform grueling work hour after hour without sufficient sleep?

- Would you push this person to the point of exhaustion and deprive him or her of food, exercise, recreation, or other basic needs?

- Would you motivate this loved one or cherished friend through harsh criticism?

The answer to these questions, of course, is always no. These questions help us to recognize, however, that there are many times when we impose these harmful expectations on ourselves. In the following sections, we discuss the importance of self-care and explore tips and exercises to help you honor your own needs as you implement the 5 Practices of the Caring Mentor.

Practical Tips for Self-Care

My mentoring journey has taught me that self-care is unique to every mentor and consists of whatever activities the individual finds healthy, nourishing, and life-affirming. The first step in caring for ourselves is to recognize the signs that indicate we need to slow down and focus attention on our own well-being. These signs include physical and mental fatigue, increased irritability or detachment, and difficulty focusing on or completing tasks.

Once we recognize these signs, self-care begins by honoring our basic physical needs. We must avoid working for extended periods without a break, allow ourselves adequate sleep, fuel the body with proper nutrition, and exercise on a regular basis. Self-care also requires us to spend time addressing our social, emotional, and psychological needs. Mentors should reach out to family and friends for companionship and support, and they should set aside time for recreation, relaxation, and fun.

My self-care takes many forms, including spending quality time with my family, enjoying long walks, meditating, eating well, getting enough sleep, listening to my favorite music, reading inspiring books, talking with friends, and traveling. In addition, I make it a point to recognize when I'm being overly self-critical and to treat myself in more loving ways through positive self-talk or by taking breaks from work. I've seen other mentors care for themselves by taking breaks throughout the day, enjoying pets and hobbies, journaling, talking about their experiences, and turning off electronic devices at prescribed times.

Another effective method of self-care is to take time to celebrate our success and appreciate our progress. Our minds have a natural tendency to gravitate toward problems because those problems often need our immediate attention. However, this may lead us to ignore the good taking place around us. To counter this, I invite mentors to make use of the following exercises.

The first exercise is for mentors to keep a thank you file and use it to save any notes from students, colleagues, or community members expressing appreciation for the mentor's work. I recommend mentors keep a physical file in their offices for handwritten notes along with a computerized file for emails and electronic documents. Rereading these messages helps mentors, especially during difficult times, remember how they've made a positive difference in the lives of others.

For the second exercise, I encourage mentors to write down everything positive that occurred in a given day and email this list to themselves before leaving work. Then, the next morning, I ask mentors to read this email before they begin any new work. This exercise trains the mind to recognize the good in our lives and work. It fosters gratitude and sets the tone for positive momentum as we start a new day.

The Caring Mentor Self-Care Action Plan

When I work with groups of mentors, I also ask them to complete the Caring Mentor Self-Care Action Plan. I invite mentors to make note of how many hours they dedicate to caring for others during a typical week. I then ask them to write down how many hours they spend caring for themselves each week. Most participants are shocked when they see the difference between these two numbers, so I ask them to write down how many hours per week they would like to dedicate to their self-care. Afterward, we discuss the definition of self-care, what self-care means to the participants, and why self-care is important.

For the next part of the exercise, I invite each member of the group to find a partner. I ask each person to identify three to five actions that they would be willing to commit to in order to support their well-being. I also ask them to identify specific days and times during the week when they can schedule these activities into their routine. After everyone has had time to complete their Caring Mentor Self-Care Action Plan, they commit to checking in with their partner every week, whether by phone, text, or email.

Mentors have shared with me that this exercise has become an essential factor in improving their well-being. When mentees record specific activities they find nourishing, set aside time for these pursuits, and ask a partner to hold them accountable, they turn a discussion about self-care into concrete action.

Below are examples of blank and completed Caring Mentor Self-Care Action Plans.

The Caring Mentor Monthly Self-Assessment Form

Blank Form

Mentor's Name: _____

Plan Date: _____

Hours I Currently Devote to Self-Care Per Week	
Hours I Will Now Devote to Self-Care Per Week	

I commit to incorporating the following self-care activities into my weekly routine on the following dates and times:

Self-Care Activity	Day(s)	Time(s)	Duration	Total Time Per Week

Name of My Self-Care Partner	Day and Time of Our Weekly Check-In

The Caring Mentor Monthly Self-Assessment Form

Completed Example

Mentor's Name: Samuel Thomas

Plan Date: January 1, 2019

Hours I Currently Devote to Self-Care Per Week	3
Hours I Will Now Devote to Self-Care Per Week	9.5

I commit to incorporating the following self-care activities into my weekly routine on the following dates and times:

Self-Care Activity	Day(s)	Time(s)	Duration	Total Time Per Week
Evening Walk	Mon-Fri	7:00 P.M.	30 Minutes	2.5 Hours
Meditation	Mon-Fri	6:30 A.M.	12 Minutes	1 Hour
Calling Friends	Saturday	11:00 A.M.	1 Hour	1 Hour
Reading	Mon-Fri	10:00 P.M.	30 Minutes	2.5 Hours
Listening to Music	Mon-Fri	7:00 A.M.	30 Minutes	2.5 Hours

Name of My Self-Care Partner	Day and Time of Our Weekly Check-In
Stephen Smith	Fridays at 5:00 P.M.

Taking the time to complete and follow through with the Caring Mentor Self-Care Action Plan helps mentors make self-care a priority. Mentors who care often have a natural inclination to put aside their own needs in order to help others. But when mentors minimize the importance of self-care, this not only has a negative effect on their health and well-being but on their performance as a mentor as well.

Suggestions for Meeting Your Own Needs through Self-Care

The following list outlines specific suggestions for meeting one's own needs as a mentor through self-care.

- Make self-care a high priority.

- Notice the signs that you are in need of self-care.

- Make time to eat well, exercise, and get sufficient sleep.

- Practice self-compassion by treating yourself in the same manner you would a loved one or cherished friend.

- Complete the Caring Mentor Self-Care Action Plan to identify healthy, nourishing, and life-affirming activities and schedule these into your daily life.

- With the help of a partner, hold one another accountable for practicing compassionate self-care on a weekly basis.

- Continue to set aside regular times for recreation, relaxation, and fun.

Bringing It All Together

We can only care effectively for others once we have cared for ourselves. Caring for ourselves is important in and of itself because it is an expression of our self-respect. I've observed that our capacity to give care is directly related to our capacity to receive care. In other words, the extent to which we can care for others depends on the degree to which we accept care for ourselves. After all, we can only give to others that which is already inside of us. If we become depleted, we have nothing left to give.

Applying the practices discussed in this chapter provide us as mentors with a solid foundation for self-care, allowing us to give our best as we implement the 5 Practices of the Caring Mentor.

CLOSING THOUGHTS

I n this final section, we explore the process of bringing mentoring relationships to a close. I also discuss a powerful way of remembering the 5 Practices of the Caring Mentor. When mentors understand these principles and put them into action, they infuse every aspect of their mentoring with care.

Bringing the Mentoring Relationship to a Close

It is normal and natural for mentoring relationships to come to an end. These relationships end at different times for different reasons. In some cases, a mentor or mentee moves or changes schools. In other cases, the relationship ends because the mentee no longer needs support, or the participants may simply have reached the time when they agreed the mentorship would end.

Regardless of how the relationship ends, mentors should bring their mentoring activities to a close with the same commitment to care that infused every other aspect of the process.

As discussed in chapter 3, mentors should end a mentoring relationship in a caring manner by letting mentees know from the start that the relationship will conclude either at a prescribed time or when mentoring is no longer needed. The end of a mentoring relationship is an opportunity to support mentees as they enter the next stage of their professional development. Mentors should arrange to meet with their mentees at a time that allows for uninterrupted conversation. As the mentoring relationship draws to a close, mentors have the opportunity to express care by helping mentees reflect on their growth, identify the lessons they have learned, and celebrate their successes. Mentors can, of course, leave the door open for future interactions if the mentee wants to stay in touch.

To end my mentoring relationships in a positive, productive, and meaningful manner, I ask mentees the following questions based on the 5 Practices:

Caring Mentor Practice #1: Caring mentors practice active listening to make a sincere connection with their mentees.
- How did the mentoring experience go for you?

- What do you consider to be the positive aspects of your mentorship? What were the areas in which you struggled?

- What are your plans for the future?

Caring Mentor Practice #2: Caring mentors create a safe place for authentic expression.

- How do you feel right now?

- How do you feel about the mentoring relationship as a whole?

- Is there anything else you'd like to share?

Caring Mentor Practice #3: Caring mentors devote themselves to their mentees' growth.

- What did you learn from our mentoring work?

- How have you grown?

- What are your professional development goals moving forward?

Caring Mentor Practice #4: Caring mentors share their perspectives and insights with their mentees.

- What insights have you gained from the mentoring process?

- How have you changed as both a person and a professional?

- What new perspectives do you have regarding your work?

Caring Mentor Practice #5: Caring mentors act on behalf of their mentees.

- How can I support your success in the future?

- Is there anything else I can do to help you as we bring the mentoring relationship to a close?

An Acronym for Remembering the 5 Practices

As I studied, applied, and shared the 5 Practices of the Caring Mentor, I wanted to develop a way for myself and others to remember these key ideas and hold them in our hearts. I use the following mnemonic device in speeches and workshops, and I hope this acronym will serve you well as you put the 5 Practices into action in your mentoring relationships.

L – Listen Actively

Taking a sincere interest in teacher and school counselor mentees begins with active listening. We give our complete attention to mentees when we put everything else aside, open our hearts and minds, and with genuine curiosity and compassion devote to our mentees the fullness of our presence. Listening to our mentees in this way builds the strong connections they need to learn and succeed.

I – Instill Safety

Being a new teacher or school counselor is difficult, to say the least. As such, our mentees experience many ups and downs as they navigate their first few years in the profession. When we offer them genuine empathy, ongoing emotional support, and a place in which they can speak freely, we instill a sense of safety in our mentees, helping them cope with the inevitable stresses that arise. We may not be able to solve every problem or understand every detail about our mentees' lives and work. We can, however, provide a safe place for their authentic expression and let them know that, whatever they are going through, they are not alone.

G – Grow Together

We also express care to our mentees by devoting ourselves to their growth and making it a priority to understand who they are, to honor their current progress, and to direct our mentoring efforts toward helping them take the next steps in their professional development. One of the most powerful ways we inspire growth in our mentees is to demonstrate our own commitment to ongoing learning and show them we are in this together.

H – Heighten Understanding

As experienced educators, we have acquired a wealth of knowledge and wisdom over the years. Part of being a caring mentor is to heighten our mentees' understanding by sharing perspectives and insights regarding who they are as teachers and school counselors. We are in a position to help them see the strengths they possess, to guide them as they share those gifts, and to help them find meaning in the process. Sharing the wisdom we possess helps us connect with our mentees socially, emotionally, and intellectually as we assist them in overcoming their challenges and offer them more beneficial ways of looking at their lives and work.

T – Take Action

Care is not limited to listening and speaking. We must take concrete actions to foster our mentees' success and bring out their best. These activities include practical assistance with daily tasks, collaborative planning, advocacy, joint projects, and other forms of action-based assistance. Mentees need the fullness of our support as new educators, and that requires us to take meaningful actions on their behalf.

LIGHT

The 5 Practices of the Caring Mentor may be remembered through the use of the acronym LIGHT. The word *light* derives from an Old English term that means "brightness, radiant energy, that which makes things visible." *Light* comes from the verb *leht*, meaning "to be luminous, bright, beautiful, shining, having much light." In other words, light is an energy that reveals the true nature of things and uncovers their potential.

The way in which the sun casts its rays on everyone, regardless of who they are or what they happen to be doing, has always inspired me. As mentors, we don't shine light on our mentees' paths because they always agree with us or live up to our expectations. We don't express loving support because our mentees are always cooperative and never make mistakes. And we don't offer the warmth of our kindness because it's convenient or because our mentees give us something in return—although, as outlined in the introduction, there are many benefits to being a caring mentor. We light the way for our mentees because they are people just like us, fellow educators and sisters and brothers in our human family. We know they have the potential to positively impact the lives of every student, colleague, and community member they meet, all the more so when offered effective, caring support.

In closing, I thank you for taking this journey with me. Together, we have learned how to put the 5 Practices of the Caring Mentor into practice within our mentoring relationships. Now that we understand how care can be given and received effectively, I'm confident we will provide our educational communities with the love and compassion they need. Together, we will leave this world a little more luminous than we found it.

L **LISTEN ACTIVELY**

Caring mentors practice active listening to make a sincere connection with their mentees.

LIGHT

INSTILL SAFETY **I**

①

Caring mentors create a safe place for authentic expression.

G **GROW TOGETHER**

Caring mentors devote themselves to their mentees' growth.

②

HEIGHTEN UNDERSTANDING **H**

③

Caring mentors share their perspectives and insights with their mentees.

T **TAKE ACTION**

Caring mentors act on behalf of their mentees.

④

⑤

SUGGESTED READING
AND RESOURCES

Bailey, Becky. *Conscious Discipline: Building Resilient Classrooms.* Oviedo: Loving Guidance, Inc., 2015.

Curran, Linda. *101 Trauma-Informed Interventions: Activities, Exercises, and Assignments to Move the Client and Therapy Forward.* Eau Claire: Premier Publishing and Media, 2013.

Cushnir, Raphael. *The One Thing Holding You Back: Unleashing the Power of Emotional Connection.* New York: HarperCollins, 2008.

Herman, Judith. *Trauma and Recovery: The Aftermath of Violence—From Domestic Abuse to Political Terror.* New York: BasicBooks, 1997.

Knowles, Malcolm. *The Adult Learner: A Neglected Species.* Houston: Gulf Publishing, 1990.

Krzyzewski, Mike. *Leading with the Heart: Coach K's Successful Strategies for Basketball, Business, and Life.* New York: Warner Books, Inc., 2001.

Lemov, Doug, and Norman Atkins. *Teach Like a Champion 2.0: 62 Techniques That Put Students on the Path to College.* San Francisco: Jossey-Bass, 2015.

Mayeroff, Milton. *On Caring.* New York: Harper & Row, 1971.

Neff, Kristin. *Self-Compassion: The Proven Power of Being Kind to Yourself.* New York: HarperCollins, 2011.

Seligman, Martin. *Learned Optimism: How to Change Your Mind and Your Life.* New York: Vintage Books, 2006.

Sinek, Simon. *Start with Why: How Great Leaders Inspire Everyone to Take Action.* New York: Portfolio/Penguin, 2009.

Sinek, Simon, and David Mead. *Find Your Why: A Practical Guide for Discovering Purpose for You and Your Team.* New York: Portfolio/Penguin, 2017.

Wooden, John. *Wooden: A Lifetime of Observations and Reflections On and Off the Court.* New York: McGraw-Hill, 1997.

Zyromski, Brett, and Melissa Mariani. *Facilitating Evidenced-Based, Data-Driven School Counseling: A Manual for Practice.* Thousand Oaks: Corwin/American School Counselor Association, 2016.

The Personal Strengths Inventory

As of the time of this writing, the Personal Strengths Inventory is free. It identifies a person's strengths within twenty-four separate categories. The assessment, which is based on the principles of positive psychology, takes approximately thirty minutes to complete. At the end, it provides a report of the respondent's strengths and their meanings. The inventory can be found at www.truity.com.

The VIA Survey of Character Strengths

Another way for individuals to discover their positive characteristics is through the VIA Survey of Character Strengths. The initial assessment, which is also free at the time of this writing, takes about fifteen minutes to complete. Participants then receive an email detailing their top strengths and have the option to purchase a more in-depth analysis. The VIA Survey of Character Strengths can be found at www.viacharacter.org.

The CliftonStrengths Assessment

The CliftonStrengths Assessment is another tool that mentees can use to understand and build upon their current strengths. While this test must be purchased, the organization behind it provides suggestions on how to apply one's strengths, as well as how to improve on one's weaknesses. The CliftonStrengths

Assessment can be found at www.gallupstrengthscenter.com/home/en-us/strengthsfinder.

Any.do

The Any.do app is an organizational tool that allows the user to create lists of goals and share them for the purpose of joint progress monitoring. This tool can be found at www.any.do.

Done: A Simple Habit Tracker

Done: A Simple Habit Tracker is another app that allows users to set goals and develop positive habits while tracking their progress. This tool can be found at www.treebetty.com.

ACKNOWLEDGMENTS

I would like to express my deep appreciation to my family. To my loving wife Mandi, throughout everything, you have always been by my side. Being your husband and sharing this life with you and our family are my greatest blessings. To my children, Myla and Benjamin, thank you for the love and joy you bring me every day. I am so very honored, grateful, and proud to be your father and so excited to support you as you pursue your own dreams. To Mom and Dad and my brother, Stephen, thank you for your unconditional support, love, and faith in me. Special thanks to Kimberly Ashley and her excellent team at The Editor Garden for their thoughtful editing and coaching. You have shown through your example what it means to be a caring mentor.

ABOUT THE AUTHOR

Daniel H. Shapiro, EdD, has served for over twenty years as a teacher, school counselor, mentor, and district leader in the Broward County Public Schools. He received National Board Teacher Certification in early adolescence/English language arts in 2006, earned his master's degree in school counseling in 2009, and received his doctoral degree in education with a specialization in instructional leadership in 2012. His doctoral dissertation was titled "An Exploration of the Role of Caring in Teacher Mentoring Relationships."

During his career, Dr. Shapiro received the Florida Governor's Shine Award for inspirational teaching. He was named a Broward County Public Schools 2014 Caliber Award winner and the 2015 Florida School Counselor Association (FSCA) Elementary School Counselor of the Year. He is now a school counseling specialist and provides mentoring and professional development to school counselors within the Broward County School District. He also serves as an adjunct professor of school counseling at Nova Southeastern University. Dr. Shapiro lives with his wife and two children in South Florida.

Contact the Author

To ask questions or request information about book sales, keynote speeches, workshops, or mentoring sessions, please contact the author, Dr. Daniel H. Shapiro, at contact@danielhshapiro.com.

CPSIA information can be obtained
at www.ICGtesting.com
Printed in the USA
LVHW080155170419
614466LV00016B/184/P